THE PLAYS OF ARNOLD WESKER

In series with this book:

THE PLAYS OF JOHN OSBORNE: an assessment
Simon Trussler

THE PLAYS
OF
ARNOLD WESKER

An Assessment

GLENDA LEEMING

AND

SIMON TRUSSLER

LONDON
VICTOR GOLLANCZ LTD
1971

Printed in Great Britain by
The Camelot Press Ltd., London and Southampton

To
LORNA AND FRED
with love and gratitude

Contents

Acknowledgements

Extracts from Arnold Wesker's works are reprinted here by kind permission of the author and Messrs Jonathan Cape. All page references in the text are to the editions of the works published by Jonathan Cape.

Our thanks are also due to Arnold Wesker, for letting us see the script of *The Friends* before its performance or publication, to Tom Maschler of Cape, for making available to us an early proof of *Fears of Fragmentation*, to Giles Gordon of Victor Gollancz Ltd, and to Carol Murphy, typist and handwriting expert *par excellence*.

INTRODUCTION

Introduction

THERE IS A wide impression that Arnold Wesker is a simple dramatist who writes simple plays—"simple" being a patronising synonym for "obvious" or "easy". Most of this simplicity is a mote in the eye of the more critical beholder, who ignores and adjusts what he sees to fit his particular preconceptions, but will be lucky if he can preserve his own simplification without foisting a lot of inconsistencies on to Wesker's works in the process. A closer examination of the plays themselves suggests a different picture: and we hope in the course of discussing their themes, characterisation, structure and language to show how superficial and deceptive the impression of simplicity really is— indeed, not only deceptive but ironic, for one of the topics to which Wesker returns most consistently is the complexity of those choices and delicate adjustments all his thinking characters have to make.

It is, of course, Wesker's undoubted but numerically rare slips into overt didacticism that supply ammunition for the attacks of his doubters. Now it is arguable that the drama can be as self-consistently didactic as it can be so much else besides: and it is not in dispute that Wesker's plays, like all other considerable works for the stage, "say" something. But because Wesker, contrary to another popular myth, does *not* choose to use the drama for propagandist purposes, on those few occasions when what is said seems out of step with what is done an audience is disconcerted by the sense that the play is stylistically off-key, rather than attentive to an interesting change of tone.

It is this incompatibility, not the relevance or otherwise of what the incidents actually proclaim, that is the real ground for condemning their occasional intrusion—that, and the targets they have set up, at which unsympathetic critics can aim generalised barbs meant to wound the works as a whole. Let it be admitted at once, then, that the incidents which most offend in this respect are Beatie Bryant's musical appreciation lesson with her mother in *Roots*, Ada Simmonds's educational game with her son in *I'm Talking About Jerusalem*, and the folk-singing episode in *Chips with Everything*.[1] Among these, at least the first and last actually make nice theatrical set-pieces, difficult though they are for actors to feel their way into and out of: but disruptive of the real force of the plays one must also confess them to be.

On the other hand, the falsely inductive argument that these short and particular passages illustrate "messages" which permeate the whole of a surrounding action should be checked at source by the nature of the plays' conclusions, most of which seem to leave audiences feeling that the work in question is saying just the opposite of what Wesker *ought* to be saying. Indeed, it is common even now to come across a playgoer or drama student unwillingly convinced that Wesker wants to prove in *Chicken Soup with Barley* that socialism can never work. After missing all the internal qualifications and problems that present themselves as the action proceeds, such an observer is ill-prepared for the characteristically open ending, which consequently he fails to connect with what he thinks he has understood.

As Kenneth Tynan once remarked of *Chips with Everything*,[2] Wesker has the power of showing what is, and at the same time conveying what might have been. The complexity that emerges from this rare ability is what Wesker seems to be identifying when he says:

> Optimism in art is the result not of happy endings and joyful exclamations but of the recognition of truths—secondary ones—whether the truth is a sad one or not.[3]

However, in examining some of Wesker's actual "endings" in relation to the total meanings of his plays, we have, on occasion, resorted to what he calls the "fatuous distinction between optimism and pessimism",[4] because the terms are broadly understood, and this is helpful when one is trying to make clear how apparent "pessimism" has really been turned inside-out to keep open "optimistic" options, however Wesker would define them.

For this reason, too, we have given the four sections into which the main part of the present study is divided our own umbrella-titles, in the belief that the labels thus assigned to the groups of plays discussed in each chapter will suggest helpful affinities rather than constricting categories. *The Kitchen* (like so many first plays at once seminal yet almost a law unto itself among Wesker's works) seemed to demand separate discussion, and this we have accorded it in the opening chapter—its title, "Daily Bread", hopefully reflecting the combination in the play itself of an almost liturgical repetition with the interminably trivial round actually being repeated. The second chapter, too, was virtually self-defining, since the so-called Wesker Trilogy—of *Chicken Soup with Barley*, *Roots* and *I'm Talking About Jerusalem*—evidently required treatment as a whole. But, as our chapter-title "Words and Silences" suggests, we have taken the connections between the plays to be more than just thematic—indeed, to relate to that inescapable but none the less vital concern of modern drama, the problem of communication, whether this consists in Ronnie or Sarah Kahn's plentiful outpourings of words or in the silences shared in mutual self-sufficiency by Dave and Ada Simmonds.

The splitting-up of Wesker's more recent work between our third and fourth chapters reflects more than just a concern with the order of its composition—although it might be as well to emphasise here that the discussion of *Their Very Own and Golden City* does follow that of *Chips with Everything* chronologically as well as logically, since the first drafts of the former play were in existence before *The Four Seasons* was conceived, even though it actually reached the stage first. *Chips with Everything* and *Golden City* reveal Wesker at his most formally discursive and episodic—to use that adjective descriptively rather than as a casual condemnation —whilst the plays are, thematically, at once studies in the potential for change, and in the fact of failure to achieve it. Thus, the first traces the failure of an upper-class central character effectively to reject the origins against which he is in truth merely in rebellion, not in revolution; and the second the failure of a son of the working-classes either to adapt successfully to the values of the establishment into which he finds himself being drawn, or to work from within for their improvement, let alone their overthrow. Again, then, both the form and theme of the plays are suggested in our composite title for the chapter in which they are discussed, "Patterns of Failure".

Wesker's next plays, *The Four Seasons* and *The Friends*, seemingly withdraw within the four walls of their settings, as if in closer reflection of their characters' "Private Pain"— a phrase Wesker has himself used[5] in distinguishing *The Four Seasons* from his earlier work, and which we have borrowed as the title of our fourth chapter. Yet although this pain is in both plays an intensely felt and genuine anguish, it cannot be divorced, as Wesker himself has made clear, from "public" preoccupations.[6] And if *The Four Seasons* makes a somewhat muted impression, for all that it is a better and more interesting piece than most of its original critics felt,[7] its rich and potentially hugely rewarding successor, *The Friends*, emerges triumphantly from the mood of malaise it has with equal assurance created, and does begin to hint at the unity between private and public living, and between life and art, that Wesker has in his non-dramatic writings been advocating with increasing conviction.

Thus, if the title of our fifth and final chapter, "Towards Totality", in which is discussed the collection of Wesker's essays and lectures published as *Fears of Fragmentation*, seems merely to spin an alliterative coin back from its flip side, the impression is not entirely misleading: for although Wesker's fears are real enough, so too are his hopes for a means of better realising the totality of human experience. And these hopes are no more outweighed by fears than, in the more conventional view of the man, are the fears by the hopes.

Although the early plays are by no means as straightforward as that conventional view has them, it must still be stressed that Wesker has developed steadily—or fairly steadily—as a dramatist from the first, not only by eliminating faults of technique, but positively, by increasing the range of his dramatic material and the certainty of his own control over it. The structural organisation of this material is both conscious and purposeful, and we shall, therefore, be especially concerned to show how Wesker's frequent use of fragmentary or episodically extended action is, far from being a beginner's sprawling experiment, intimately related to his specific subject-matter. Equally, the more closely-concentrated actions serve their own, quite distinct purposes: so that although George Devine wanted Wesker to concentrate into one the first two acts of the already compact *Roots*, the dramatist was right to insist that its leisurely development was more of the essence of the play than a neatly unfolding plot-line.[8]

Structurally, then, it is one argument of the present work that from *The Kitchen* onwards, but more particularly after the writing of the Trilogy, Wesker has learnt more fully to exploit the possibilities of the chronicle form in the short interacting scenes of *Chips with Everything* and *Their Very Own and Golden City*: and that he has then, after experimenting with a symmetrical, four-part schema in *The Four Seasons*, proceeded in *The Friends* successfully to shape an action which evolves during less than twenty-four hours in a one-room setting, and in which, for all its return to the brief time-span of *The Kitchen*, there is as little sense of artificial contrivance as if he had perfected his craft in no other kind of play.

Stylistically, too, the command over language in the plays increases from the functional competence of *The Kitchen*, with its polyglot kaleidoscope of accents, and from the instinctive verbal exuberance of the Kahns in *Chicken Soup*. Already in *Roots* and *Jerusalem* subtler, more evocative effects are discernible, and in *Golden City* and *The Friends* many passages achieve a theatrical lyricism of their own, in a perfect, synoptic expression of fused thought and feeling. To some extent this stylistic development is the most salient feature of Wesker's progress as a dramatist to date, but in effect—since their language is not something applied to the plays externally or decoratively—it reflects the maturity of thought and technique that also helps to affirm his status as a major world playwright.

To the extent that this is not a fashionable evaluation, the assessment of Wesker's work which follows is a corrective one: that is, certain of its emphases are dictated by the necessity to challenge impressions that might, had nobody ever written a word about his plays before, have appeared so perverse as not to need pre-emptive correction. More positively, it seemed important to look at some of the less noticed virtues of the Trilogy, to reconsider the prevailing tendency to praise *Their Very Own and Golden City* with faint damns, and to devote considerable space to an analysis of *The Friends*, in view of its generally unfavourable critical reception and of the unsatisfactory production by Wesker himself which in part prompted this.[9]

It should be emphasised, however, that like *The Plays of John Osborne*, the first work in the present series, this study pretends neither to be a glorified review of the plays in performance, nor a literary assessment of texts which are fixed forever between the covers of a printed volume. Rather, it is a commentary upon and an evaluation of the plays as working scripts, open to all manner of interpretations, whether these are at the inspiration of director, actors or audiences—who each respond to and enrich a performance with their own moods and insights. Thus, we don't consider that these plays should be pinned-down in perpetuity by now fragmentary impressions of two or three productions, still less that they are adequately accessible in the privacy of the printed word: an imaginative translation must, then, always be made from page to stage, so that their full potential can be visualised in the forming of the reader's or director's platonic ideal of a performance or tested against next week's hopeful stab by the local rep with equal usefulness.

It's worth adding that critical works which *do* set out to evaluate plays in terms of particular performances are, conversely, themselves most valuable when they concentrate on points of production and don't pass judgement on the text. Indeed, they tend to be positively misleading when the one element begins to be mistaken for the other, as in one critic's very widely circulated belief that nobody but Joan

Plowright could make Beatie Bryant's climactic speech in *Roots* work on stage—an assertion that looked singularly wrong and rather shabby when it was allowed to stand in a revised edition published well after Bridget Turner's quite different but equally persuasive performance in the Royal Court revival.[10]

We have worked brief plot-synopses into our early remarks on each play, but these are intended to jog memories rather than to substitute summary for substance. It is for this reason that we have given page-references to the texts of the plays,[11] in square brackets immediately after each quotation or allusion: this is a bit unsightly, but it should enable the reader to follow our commentary in close conjunction with his set of playscripts, the better either to substantiate or dispute it. References other than those to the plays have been kept to a minimum, and have been gathered together in the first of the appendices at the back of the book: others provide a brief chronology of Wesker's career as a playwright, a complete set of cast-lists of London productions and revivals of his plays, and a bibliography of work by and about the dramatist.

And then, slipped in unobtrusively between the opinionated body of the book and these factual appendages, comes the inappropriately named conclusion. To pretend to sum up what can at best be an interim assessment of a living dramatist's work—a mere dozen years or so of a working lifetime—is in itself impertinent, and for this reason the section is a short one. Thankfully, one's feelings about Wesker's future—though infected by his own fears for contemporary society and its priorities—are the more hopeful for his own clarity of intention and, increasingly, his assurance of method. If this book helps to affirm the reputation of a writer who has suffered by his determination not to follow every latest fashion in playwriting or politicking, but to let his own vision mature—and bravely, albeit abortively, also to test it against harsh practicalities in the Centre Fortytwo project, which even caused him to abandon for a while a more certain if not necessarily truer vocation—then it will have been well worth the writing.

THE PLAYS OF ARNOLD WESKER

I

Daily Bread

The Kitchen

ALTHOUGH SOME OF Wesker's later plays—notably *Their Very Own and Golden City* and *The Friends*—went through several drafts before seeing performance or print, only *The Kitchen* has actually been both staged and published[12] in differing versions. Of these, the earlier and shorter was performed at the Royal Court as a production-without-decor on 13th September 1959, and the revised, more substantial script was given its first performance on 27th June 1961, in a limited run at the same theatre. It is this second version which will be discussed here, since the additions made by Wesker—which make the piece about a quarter as long again—amplify rather than modify one's feelings about the original. Anyway, to over-elucidate textual niceties would be to deny space to the real, substantive complexities of the play.

Suffice it here, then, to note the more important changes, of which the first is a detailed elaboration of the expository dialogue. This sets the scene of the play in the "large kitchen in a restaurant called the Tivoli" [5]—a place evidently geared to prefabricated, mass-production feeding—and introduces the cooks, who slowly drift to their stations as the time to prepare for the hectic lunchtime service approaches. Then, as the pace rapidly accelerates, Wesker substitutes for the originally brief glimpse of the waitresses and cooks working at full stretch to keep up with the demands of the dining-room, what amounts to a libretto for the more detailed orchestration of comings-and-goings which John Dexter worked out in production for this complicated but very necessary episode. And, lastly, the contrast to all these comings and goings that one senses during the play's "interlude"—which, if the playwright's wish that his work be performed without an interval is honoured, immediately follows the "barking-raving-bloody-mad" conclusion to the first part [51]—is more clearly pointed and better sustained.

Even this interlude—which fades imperceptibly into the second part as the action approaches the slightly more leisurely evening service—is set in the kitchen itself, from which several of the cooks are too exhausted or too far from home to attempt a short afternoon's escape. For "the kitchen is always there". [13] And its everyday routine of humdrum work, casually-sparked squabbles and snatched respite—a routine only varied in the play by those few deliberately more dramatic moments which contribute to its forceful climax— really makes up the substance of the action. In this way *The Kitchen* is at once realistic and representative: for a director's ability to contain an action that so nearly approaches documentary realism in its details of kitchen routine within a form that verges upon the expressionistic—especially in its manner of relating the place's overwhelmingly mechanistic trappings to the human responses these shape and provoke— has tended to determine the success of the play in production.

It has been argued[13] that no kitchen in any restaurant has ever resembled that of Wesker's Tivoli: and some of the items on its evidently lengthy menu are not perhaps of the kind one would expect to be churned out on a gastronomic assembly line at the alleged rate of two thousand a day. [23] But even if one doesn't allow Wesker, with some four years' experience of such places,[14] to know better than his critics in this case, given the formal assumptions underpinning the play the incongruity scarcely matters. The Tivoli is not just a kitchen: it is, eponymously, *the* kitchen—and microcosmic, maybe, of the society it serves. Comments Wesker:

> The world might have been a stage for Shakespeare but to me it is a kitchen, where people come and go and cannot stay long enough to understand each other, and friend-ships, loves and enmities are forgotten as quickly as they are made. [5]

And here, Peter, the German cook who comes closest to being the play's central character, emphasises the place's omnipresence:

> This—this madhouse it's always here. When you go, when I go, when Dimitri go—this kitchen stays. It'll go on when we die, think about that. We work here—eight hours a day, and yet—it's nothing. We take nothing. Here —the kitchen, here—you. You and the kitchen. And the kitchen don't mean nothing to you and you don't mean to the kitchen nothing. [53]

Peter has a naturally explosive and erratic temperament: and this, of course, is exaggerated by the strain of the con-ditions in which he works. Similarly, it is both a "real" consequence of the heat and noise of the kitchen and func-tionally appropriate to the play that the other cooks' characteristics should, under pressure, be heightened to a greater or lesser extent. "All kitchens, especially during service, go insane," remarks Wesker, [5] and even the least assertive of the cooks he has created, Michael, is said to be "infused with a kind of madness" that is common to his profession. [8]

Like Michael, each of the characters, from Marango the proprietor—for whom the kitchen is a kind of umbilical extension of himself—to Mangolis the kitchen porter, and from the chef to the new waitress, is given his or her potted biography in the printed text of the play. [7–9] Indeed, all the nuances and slight differentiations of character Wesker specifies might at first seem superfluous in a work in which it is of the essence that conditions have imposed at best a superficiality and at worst a complete impersonality upon human relations—a play in which, furthermore, no single character apart from Peter among the thirty-odd mentioned by name in the cast-list is dramatically much more dominant than any other.

Yet one point of the larger-than-life manner in which the nature of their environment forces the characters to put across their feelings is precisely that it is larger than *life*: there are individual and, in close analysis, clearly discernible traits which make their own inflation into Jonsonian humours consistent and believable. For an audience, the characters can only live inside the kitchen—the more so since a good portion of their leisure time falls in the afternoon, and so is also passed in or under the shadow of the place. The kitchen at once demands and dramatically displays the time and energies of its employees, and the closeness of its confines, creating a theatrically vivid image, overshadows even their few recollections of activity on the margins of days and ways. Even the necessity for miming much of the practical business of the place becomes a positive virtue in this respect, since the effect here is of distancing, and thus of increasing one's awareness of the nature of operations which are, so far as they go, utterly realistic, yet, because they stop short of all the trimmings, also stylised.

There are thus three factors which contribute to one's impression of the kitchen-as-madhouse: but of these, the

most clearly manifest—the actual behaviour of the characters—is arguably no more than a consequence of a conditioning process the two others have combined to perpetuate.
However, behaviour-under-pressure itself *becomes* an active
agency for feeding the frantic climate to which it was originally a response: so that, in the action as we witness it, cause
and effect are virtually inseparable. Dramatically almost as
dominant, though easier to overlook in approaching the
play as script rather than production, are firstly the physical
oppressiveness of the kitchen as a place with a predatory life
of its own, and secondly, permeating everything, the continuous noise of the ovens.

Although, as Wesker notes, "any producer is at liberty
to abstract" the set, if he "can still get over the atmosphere", [7] it *is* vital that this atmosphere should reflect
upon and be reflected in the more personalised action. Thus,
the peak of activity reached during the lunchtime service at
the close of the first part soaks up all personal responses into
itself: human activity is caught up in and becomes a part of
the mechanistic process, and an audience must be aware of
the kitchen as such in this consummation of its purpose. But
when, during the interlude, the pressure is briefly eased and
"the ovens are low", [57] the resultant shift in dramatic
emphasis, effective theatrically because it is so strongly
marked, becomes most discernible in a tentative humanising
of relationships. This the characters themselves sense, and
here the Jewish pastrycook Paul, always the most articulate,
puts the feeling into words, addressed to the dislikeable
Peter:

> Now it's quiet, the ovens are low, the work has stopped for
> a little and now I'm getting to know you. I still think
> you're a pig—only now, not so much of a pig. So that's
> what I dream. I dream of a friend. You give me a rest,

you give me silence, you take away this mad kitchen so I make friends, so I think—maybe all the people I thought were pigs are not so much pigs. [57]

The evening service which follows the interlude is comparatively more relaxed than the lunchtime one: but because of this, instead of sensibilities being sublimated in meeting the demands of the moment, tempers are frayed by them. There is more time for talking, and therefore for the arguments into which talk here always devolves. But on this particular evening a waitress's ill-considered insult combines with an apparently determined repulse from his mistress Monique to drive Peter to a pitch of frenzy—and to drive the large chopper he seizes (intent on destroying property, not persons) into the gas main. There is "a slow hiss and all the fires of the ovens die down". And the "second of complete silence before anybody realises what has happened" [76] is a theatrical moment of tremendous force, both in it necessary emotional catharsis, and, cerebrally, in one's dawning awareness of how silence differs in quality from that perpetual drone of the ovens to which an audience has become so accustomed as to go almost unnoticed, but which is an essential and, for the cooks, inescapable part of their daily lives.

It needs to be emphasised that only in Peter's gesture of frustration and defiance against his mistress, his condition, and the kitchen itself, does this day differ in tenor from any other. The points of dramatic emphasis—the arrival in the morning of a new cook, Kevin, an accidental scalding, a long and important speech by Paul towards the end of the interlude, and, pervasively, the simmering quarrel between Peter and Monique—arise naturally from the normal rhythms of the kitchen's routine, into which the characters themselves slip instinctively, as from long habit. It is thus also notable that it should not be by any especially traumatic development in Peter's relationship with Monique that his frenzy is prompted. True, the girl's apparently increasing preference for the undemanding security her husband offers her, as against the trials of her tempestuous love for Peter, is a strong contributing factor. But it is the trivial-seeming tiff with a waitress—who helps herself to turbot from Peter's station instead of waiting her turn to be served—that precipitates his violent reaction. The *kitchen* provokes it, and the kitchen bears its brunt.

This incident is important in at least three ways. Firstly, and dramatically most important, in giving an otherwise intentionally humdrum action a satisfying theatrical shape and a felt climax. Secondly, in terms of characterisation, as a physical gesture against his environment that has long been sublimated in Peter's verbal irritability, and in aggression turned against his fellow-employees rather than the force which oppresses them all. And thirdly, in terms of the false assumptions about humanity and human behaviour which the place countenances and reinforces: assumptions which have to do both with the function of work itself in the life of man, and with the various antagonisms—personal, functional, racial—that this particular work has sparked.

If the play has a discernible theme, it is surely here. And, significantly, it has to do once again with the kitchen as simultaneously a dramatic metaphor for industrial capitalist society, and a very specific and closely specified place. Consider the integration of these levels in the particular insult of the waitress's that finally infuriates Peter beyond endurance. "You Boche you," she mutters under her breath. "You bloody German bastard!" [76] Now this isn't merely a reach-me-down device of a dramatist in search of a motive: it is part of the quiet yet insistent undercurrent of racialism that seems to infect most members of the kitchen staff, of whatever race they happen to be themselves. And even in this particular, the kitchen is at once larger-than-life in its representational capacity and utterly true to itself: for the kitchen of a large London restaurant *will* almost invariably draw upon a broader cross-section of racial types than most places of work, and at the same time it *will* thus become a boiling pot in which generally separate and separable kinds of racial tension are to be found in a confused agglomeration.

English, Irish, Germans, Italians, Cypriots, Maltese, Jews —all mix here naturally and, within their own marked-out areas of interest and precedence, more or less amicably. But whereas most of his fellow-Cypriots, like Mangolis, are kitchen porters, the temperamental Gaston is a cook—and the first quarrel of which we hear is caused by Peter having called him a "lousy Cypro" on the previous day. [17] That Peter should feel free to fling such insults whilst reacting so violently to the later slur on his own nationality is, of course, also a point whose individual irony contributes to the play's dramatic shape, yet which remains utterly typical of the confused racialist mentality. And similar unthinking assumptions of racial inferiority are scattered throughout the play—the Jewish vegetable cook Bertha telling the Cypriot Nicholas that "the lavatory is your country", and getting called a foreigner herself for her pains, [23] or the Irish Kevin remarking in sour surprise upon his discovery that such a decent fellow as Paul should be a Jew.

The taciturn butcher Max has, for that matter, already called Peter "a bloody German" earlier that day—out of his hearing, admittedly, but tossing the insult about with the easy abandon of custom. So that while the importance of these racial slanging-matches—other than the one that proves climactic—should not be over-emphasised, they are the more *right* in that, whilst giving the closing row its proper context, the characters do not themselves regard them as important or take them very seriously. Racial abuse is no more than a matter of give and take: except that just occasionally it becomes a matter of life and death.

That Paul should be both a Jew and a pastrycook tempts one into thinking of him as Wesker's mouthpiece: this would be too easy an identification, but it is true that *functionally* Paul does have, along with his fellow pastrycook Raymond, at least something of an observer's role. For, as Wesker notes, these two are professionally less caught up in the panic of the kitchen, their work more regularly paced. [9] So if Paul seems temperamentally more of a talker than his fellow-workers, this may be partly because his less taxing job gives his tongue freer rein. Once again, the elements of individual character-building, of dramatic purpose, and of function within the kitchen itself are inextricable. So too the Cypriots, regarded as racially inferior, are handed out the inferior jobs, thus both perpetuating the myth of their inferiority and, perforce, giving substance to its actuality.

It is Paul who most clearly articulates the wider implications of *The Kitchen*, as play and as place, in its longest and arguably most crucial speech. During the relative peace of the interlude, Peter, with characteristic sudden enthusiasm and overriding insistence upon involving others in a new idea, demands that everybody "tell us a dream". [55] Dimitri dreams of a workshop of his own, Kevin dreams simply of sleep, the young German cook Hans of money, Raymond of women. But Paul refuses to join in—or rather reveals his own dream, of friendship, in a roundabout way, in his story of a next-door neighbour who is a bus driver and of their originally casual, undemanding relationship:

> Then one day the busmen go on strike. He's out for five weeks. Every morning I say to him, "Keep going mate, you'll win." Every morning I give him words of

B

encouragement; I say I understand his cause. I've got to get up earlier to get to work but I don't mind. We're neighbours. We're workers together, he's pleased. Then, one Sunday, there's a peace march. I don't believe they do much good but I go, because in this world a man's got to show he can have his say. The next morning he comes up to me and he says, now listen to this, he says "Did you go on that peace march yesterday?" So I says Yes, I did go on that peace march yesterday. So then he turns round to me and he says, "You know what? A bomb should have been dropped on the lot of them! It's a pity," he says, "that they had children with them cos a bomb should've been dropped on the lot!" And you know what was upsetting him? The march was holding up the traffic, the buses couldn't move so fast! Now I don't want him to say I'm right, I don't want him to agree with what I did, but what terrifies me is that he didn't stop to think that this man helped me in my cause so maybe, only *maybe*, there's something in his cause. I'll talk about it. No! The buses were held up so drop a bomb he says, on the lot! [58]

The language here—its repetitive use of phrases which at one moment ring colloquially true, at the next rhetorically effective; its use of connective or of interruptive words to introduce continuing or segmentary thoughts; its very slightly non-idiomatic or consciously idiomatic flavour—is typical of Wesker's success in *The Kitchen* in making purposeful use of his polyglot cast list. But most important is *what* Paul is saying. Like the servicemen and office girls who disgust Dave and Ada Simmonds in *Chicken Soup with Barley*, [41] the busman and his like seem separated off from Paul by a failure of sympathy so impenetrable that a mixture of despair of ever shifting such a dead weight of incompre-

hension, and of sickened distaste for even attempting the
effort of communication, necessarily infects many of Wesker's
originally optimistic characters. Of these, Paul is the first to
find that his dream is a nightmare.

What prevents a simple elitist solution—or resignation—
emerging in consequence from Wesker's plays is the centrality
of *environment* to the problem. Paul himself is infected by his
surroundings, even in so slight a matter as his refusal of a
cake to Michael. As he reflects afterwards:

> Doesn't hurt me to give him a cake, most times we do but
> there's always that one time when we don't. First thing in
> the morning I joke with him and half way through the
> day I lie to him, defending the governor's property as
> though it was me own. I don't know what to be bloody
> loyal to half the time. [37]

But of course Paul's speculative, deductive recognition here
of the implications of the incident—his ability to make the
connections—helps to counteract its effects upon him. For
those such as Paul's bus driver, on the other hand, there is
dislocation not only between various of their own thoughts,
but between their own and anybody else's point of view.

"And the horror is this," as Paul himself puts it, "that
there's a wall, a big wall between me and millions of people
like him." But he himself recognises the importance of *place*
in the moulding of these millions:

> I look around me, at the kitchen, at the factories, at the
> enormous bloody buildings going up with all those offices
> and all those people in them, and I think, Christ! I
> think, Christ, Christ, Christ! [58]

Thus, while Paul's millions may unconsciously allow some

of the deformities of the system to infect them, they are not themselves wholly or decisively to blame for these deformities. Attitudes towards the seemingly impenetrable inertia of the working class are not reducible here, or elsewhere in Wesker's plays, to the dismissive, but continue to oscillate between exasperated sympathy and furious revulsion, in the consciousness of being caught in just this vicious circle.

Neither are simplistic solutions to the reform of an evidently rotten society possible or proposed. For it is on this final questioning note that Paul's interlude story ends:

But then I think: I should stop making pastries? The factory worker should stop making trains and cars? The miner should leave the coals where it is . . . ? *You* give *me* an answer. You give me your dream. [58–9]

And so Dimitri works in a kitchen, instead of a factory producing the wireless sets he loves to tinker with at home, because "in a factory a man makes a little piece till he becomes a little piece, you know what I mean?" [19] Yet without the men making those separate little pieces for a living, Dimitri couldn't fit them all together for fun. And such kitchens as the Tivoli's—for feeding the masses quickly and cheaply—are not all that different from a factory in their deadening routines and debilitating working conditions.

Marango, the Tivoli's proprietor, pins down most exactly this central paradox of the play, elaborated though it is more diffusely during the dreaming sequence, when he asks, at the very end:

I don't know what more to give a man. He works, he eats, I give him money. This is life, isn't it? I haven't made a mistake, have I? I live in the right world, don't I . . . ?

What is there more? What is there more? What is there more? [78–9]

"We have seen," Wesker's stage direction to the original version added, "that there must be something more."[15] But it does not lie merely in smartening up this particular kitchen, so as to give creative cookery and what it represents a chance:

> KEVIN: You'd've thought it was possible to run a small restaurant that could take pride in its food and made money too.
> PETER: Of course it's possible, my friend—but you pay to eat in it. It's money. It's all money. The world chase money so you chase money too. [39]

And, as Paul has pointed out, unless some saner system is evolved, simply to destroy or opt out of the kitchen world will—as Sarah Kahn and Libby Dobson assert during the Trilogy, and as Dave and Ada Simmonds find out the hard way—only starve the real needs that kitchen, factory and office in their grinding monotony supply.

Dimitri, although rejecting the dehumanising factory routine, himself points out the almost identical effects of work in the kitchen:

> Listen, you put a man in the plate-room all day, he's got dishes to make clean, and stinking bins to take away, and floors to sweep, what else is there for him to do—he wants to fight. He got to show he is a man some way. So —blame him! [19]

The conflicts, whether dramatic, personal or social, resolve themselves only into this irreconcilability between man and a setting that diminishes his humanity. The overwhelming heat, speed, noise, smells and curtailed or elliptic human interactions of the kitchen illustrate in the course of the play just how little the very different personalities of the polyglot staff mean or matter in the pursuit of meal-mongering—and again it is Paul who makes the environmental association, asserting "when the world is filled with kitchens you get pigs". [57] Even Peter betrays his own instant ideal of dream spinning, explaining, evasively but reasonably, "I can't dream in a kitchen." [70]

Since circumstances combine to grind the characters down to the uniformity of their functions, it is all the more remarkable that one can sense the underlying differences between individuals even when these are most completely submerged in the grind of routine. Peter, of course, is most clearly individualised, and the strength of his characterisation lies in its very unattractiveness, hysterical-sounding laugh and all. Even the boy's redeeming features—such as his gift of cutlets to a tramp under the noses of his superiors in the second part [68]—are attributable not so much to generosity as to an impetuosity that can as readily make him perverse or cruel. And as Monique's lover he seems both selfish and assertive even in his real desperation.

The relatively humane qualities of Paul thus become the more necessary—if only in alleviation of the otherwise mordant dramatic tone, and, of course, also as an intellectual counterbalance to the prevailing poverty of thinking the kitchen induces. The kitchen porter Dimitri, too, has a sense of priorities such as might shame his supposed superiors—but he is the better balanced character for not assuming the assertive Common Man role a lesser dramatist than Wesker might have considered obligatory to a job dealing with humanity's dregs and leftovers.

If Wesker does not tread so surely in his handling of sexual relationships—the relevance of Paul's failed marriage, introduced only into the longer version of the play, is never clear, and Peter and Monique do sometimes talk as if they'd never met before—his handling of the casual, almost imperceptible male relationships on the sidelines of the action is, however, clear and assured. The grudging father-son feelings between Max and Nicholas, the hierarchical distancing between the senior chefs and the junior, even the friendly arrangement fixed up between Paul and Raymond for mending the former's motor bike during an evening's work and pleasure—all have the tang of truth about them. This last incident was also introduced only into the longer version of the play, and—one might mention several additional wise-cracking lines given to Bertha, the fat vegetable cook—is typical of the locally-colourful nature of the minor additions to the text.

Then there is Frank, a former prisoner-of-war, now second chef, his sensibilities successfully deadened by drink. And the Chef himself, hating the responsibility that goes along with his better pay, passing the buck if he can and pretending not to notice if he can't. And poor pimply Hans, callow yet sensitive. And easy-going Anne, working away quietly on the desserts and coffees. And finally—the functions of this pair much more purposeful in relation to the theme of the play—there are the two characters who, if *The Kitchen* had been expressionistic in characterisation as well as in mood and setting, might well have been called The Worker and The Boss.

Alfredo, about sixty-five, is a cook—and a worker—cast in traditional mould, who despises his work, but gets on with it all the same because that is what workers are meant to do. Peter suggests, ironically, that Kevin should imitate his example:

Be like Mr Alfredo. Nothing disturbs Mr Alfredo. Mr

Alfredo is a worker and he hates his boss. He knows his
job but he does no more no less and at the right time. Mr
Alfredo is an Englishman. . . . [39]

None the less real for his typicality is Marango, the boss
Alfredo hates—perplexed that more can be expected of him
than good pay, or less of his staff than the same dedication
that has made his kitchen synonymous with his own existence. "The machine he has set in motion is his whole life,"
comments Wesker, "and he suspects that everyone is con-
spiring to stop it." [9]

Eventually, of course, Peter does stop it, and brings the
play, too, to an end. This incident apart, Marango's world
duly revolves on its axis every twenty-four hours, the inexor-
able sameness of each day's trivial round implied in the
representative working-day spanned by the play itself, which
creates its own self-contained and infinitely repeatable
rhythm. This circular structure one might compare with
that of *Waiting for Godot*—if it contained within it even such
a false hope of redemption as Godot represents, or if one
were not aware that a ruptured gas main was demonstrably
an inadequate augury of his arrival.

Much later in Wesker's dramatic career, *Chips with
Everything* was to share with *The Kitchen* its style of modified
(almost ritualised) naturalism, as well as its compact,
potentially repetitive cylical structure—in strong contrast
with the indefinitely developing, episodically flowing *Chicken
Soup with Barley*, *I'm Talking About Jerusalem* or *Their Very
Own and Golden City*. The cycles of both plays—respectively
of the working day, and of the eight-week period of basic
military training—are recognisable as external constraints
upon the characters, representative, though in unusually
well-defined form, of all those constraints of society which
impose soul-destroying patterns on people's lives. And in so

far as a single day is the more familiar—and, dramatically, more conventionalised—cycle of the two, its acceptability to an audience as a representative unit in a predetermined pattern is the more assured.

The effect of this assurance is to stress the difficulty of escaping from the kitchen world. As Paul asks, "What do you do about it?" [58] And as Marango asks, "What is there more?" [79] No answers are offered in the play,[16] and the sombreness of its vision, as of so much of Wesker's work, strikes one all the more forcibly when this is compared with the positive conclusion of *Roots*. That play was to end as its protagonist found herself jolted by a failed love-affair into a full realisation of the priorities and influences shaping her life—including those of the society that had been insidiously conditioning her. But in a similarly climactic position in *The Kitchen*, Peter's jilting by Monique impels him to an act of destruction which, although aimed at the kitchen, is no more than an instinctive emotional response, merely more intense than his usual anger at this or that aspect of his own or his comrade's conditions. It is a violent gesture, made in the right direction[17]—but offering no such advance as Dimitri feels to be the only hope:

Sometimes things happen and no one sees the point— and then suddenly, something else happen and you see the point. Peter not a fool! You not a fool! People's brain moves all the time. *All* the time, I'm telling you. [60]

Bewilderment, lack of vision, disillusionment: on their own, these do not necessarily add up to inflexible pessimism. The added imposition of a cyclical time scheme does, however, tend to direct one's overall response to the play towards pessimism, by discouraging the hope of freer choices ever swinging the action on to another course.

But discouragement may not have been what Wesker intended: for the more flexible development of his next three plays does leave, even if only by implication, alternative courses open, and the possibilities of making them more hopeful.

Words and Silences

Chicken Soup with Barley, Roots
and *I'm Talking About Jerusalem*

THERE IS AS much surface pessimism in *Chicken Soup with Barley*—which had its first productions in Coventry and London in July 1958, and opened the repertory season of the Wesker Trilogy at the Royal Court just two years later—as in any other of Wesker's naturalistic plays, and the spiritual course of its action arcs steadily downwards. In 1936, as the play opens, the Kahn family, Sarah and Harry and their children, the fourteen-year-old Ada and her younger brother Ronnie, form part of a like-minded East End Jewish community, joining in concerted anti-fascist action in Cable Street. But by the immediate post-war period of the second act, only Sarah and Ronnie still retain their original socialist inspiration. Harry's wavering commitment has sunk into an apathy to which he is soon physically harnessed by his first stroke, and Ada, with her husband Dave, retreats from a world that doesn't seem worth reforming. Finally, in the third act, rare visits from past neighbours—who have either come to accept the status quo, or choose to ignore it—spotlight the distance the Kahns have come from the thronged basement of the first act: and Ronnie returns from Paris to attack Sarah with his own loss of socialist faith in the wake of the Hungarian uprising of 1956.

Pointedly, Ronnie's final anti-epiphany repeats the pattern of Ada's second-act alienation, and even the ebullient first act is retrospectively ironic—its confident, unfulfilled hopes and predictions culminating in the ominous domestic quarrel between Sarah and Harry. Monty Blatt's last-act comment, "It's all come to this," is no revelation; [64] ten years earlier, in the dawn of the brave new welfare state, Harry had already been proclaiming that he was an old man, too old to change. Fallings away from faith mark almost every scene up to Ronnie's culminating apostasy; and these fallings away are inseparable from the playwright's vision, qualifying the determinedly, desperately straightforward vision of the undeviating Sarah Kahn.

The dilemma, of choosing between the possibly sterile preservation of a pure ideal, and the defilement perhaps inseparable from effective compromise, has proved over and over again a fruitful and magnetically attractive dramatic subject, especially to Wesker. It is provocative to playwright and audience, provided the simplistic critic does not try to resolve it by main force, and so amputate its complexities. Here, certain elements in the development of the dilemma, such as the tendency to weakness passed on from father to son, or the last-act confrontation between a mother and a son returned in despair from Paris, are even reminiscent of the works of another dramatist, equally fascinated by the ideal-compromise problem, Henrik Ibsen. In particular, as these parallels suggest, the similarities between *Chicken Soup* and *Ghosts* are striking. Both sons return in stricken resentment to their homes, and both mothers hear those sons reject the ideals they have taught them. Oswald Alving's father has bequeathed his son a physical corruption stemming from self-indulgence, which, seesaw-like, tips liberal Oswald into an invalid's rapaciously self-indulgent hedonism: whilst Harry Kahn by the end of Wesker's play has transmitted his moral enervation, though not yet his bodily paralysis, to his son Ronnie.

Of course, Sarah has to combat a self-centredness which is manifested in Harry's lethargy, not in Captain Alving's excessive animal spirits; and whereas Oswald grudges Mrs Alving's apparent neglect, Ronnie resents Sarah's benevolent domestic matriarchy. And differences of technique are more significant: characteristically, Wesker displays the struggles of the older Kahns at discursive length over several decades, whilst *Ghosts* more nearly approaches a "well-made" unity, confining its action to a few days, and encapsulating past events in exposition-cum-reminiscence. This indicates not just Wesker's less formally-confined approach to his subject, but, motivating this, his interest in and estimate of the importance of a gradual, unobtrusive development.

For the same reason, *Chicken Soup* avoids such sensational ingredients as the venereal disease and euthanasia which once so confused Ibsen's issues. The Cable Street demonstration is subordinate to the character drawing, unlike the orphanage fire in *Ghosts*, which functions both as an ostentatious symbol and as a major plot development. And the respectively medial and climactic positions of Harry's and Oswald's pathetic collapses similarly reveal Wesker playing down dramatic effects where Ibsen was playing them up.

One of the lights which *Ghosts* casts on *Chicken Soup* does, however, illuminate a crux of the play: the question of whose drama it is. Oswald engrosses the active suffering of *Ghosts* and disintegrates into the limelight of the play's last few lines; but as the character who is simply present throughout the action, who makes crucial choices, and who is complex and developing, Mrs Alving has the pivotal role. Similarly Ronnie's dramatic last-act appearance in *Chicken Soup* is only in its theatrical emphasis weightier than Ada's defiance

in act two, whilst it is Sarah Kahn who is at the true centre
of the play.[18] It is not her *tragedy*, certainly—the point being
that she does *not* undergo a tragic fall even in the form of
personal despair. Yet not only does her standing firm as other
characters fall away give her a relative dramatic motion, but
this effort of steadfastness is in itself a dynamic act—a
fight, she calls it—against the temptation to lapse into indifference, and against the actual indifference of her friends.

It is easy but deceptive to take the other characters'
estimate of Sarah as authoritative. Monty Blatt has a ready
explanation. "For her the world is black and white. If
you're not white so you must be black. She can't see shades
in character—know what I mean? She can't see people in
the round." [62] Monty's Sarah sounds like a stereotype
intended to be a stereotype. But any such impression is
inconsistent with her last long speeches to Ronnie. Her own
doubts are not in fact bundled out of the way. Ambiguously
she had asked, as Monty blamed his disillusion on atrocity
stories about Russia, "And you believe the stories now,
Monty?" [62] To Ronnie, however, she later admits "You
think it doesn't hurt me—the news about Hungary . . . ?
Who do I know who to trust now—God, who are our friends
now?" [74–5]

But because she still holds at least by the ideal she knows
to be good—whereas Monty's not dissimilar doubt "I'm
too small; who can I trust?" [62] had enabled him simply
to opt out of his difficulties—it is paradoxically Sarah who
has made the more complex political adjustment, and Monty
who has rejected all the shades of grey because they are not
white. In effect, then, when Sarah asks "If the electrician
who comes to mend my fuse blows it instead, so I should stop
having electricity? I should cut off my light?" [75] She
is choosing, rhetorically, the hopefully socialist way of life,
suffering with her eyes open the often brutal inadequacies

of fellow humans like her husband. The play's title is an unobtrusive affirmation that, for all that there is a dead weight of men like Harry, there are also women like Mrs Bernstein [75] with the chicken soup that once saved Ada's life. And though Harry's selfishness has been aggravated by his close relationship to the family he left, Mrs Bernstein's kindness is the greater for being disinterested. Sarah, then, cares not because she refuses to face discouraging facts, but because she *must*—by an effort of will.

Disillusionment is a danger when any idealistic system of politics, philosophy or religion is tested against practicalities, because the perfect vision is always so distant from the behaviour of the imperfect men who must be its agents and its material. Crudely, then, disillusion succeeds the opening of a credibility gap. The younger Kahns experience this, as do others like Monty Blatt and Dave Simmonds, and the serious impoverishment caused by such a loss of faith must be dramatically anticipated and reinforced by their absolute involvement and sincerity in the opening scene. Although the irony mentioned above hovers in act one, "when all the world was a communist", [74] over the intoxicating victory against the fascists, as it does over Monty's "I bet we have a revolution soon," [25] the characters themselves are totally identified with their cause, in a kind of holy fervour: and subsequent bitterness, even if it be concealed, is directly proportionate to the cause's deep meaning for them at that point.

At the beginning Harry contains the irreconcilables within himself, the irreproachable theory of "I tell you, show a young person what socialism means and he recognises life! A future!" [31] set against his own lackadaisical practice. And so, in this way the opposite of Sarah, he has no tightrope to walk between the two: for he is protected on the one hand by procrastinatory long-sightedness—"But it won't be pure

a socialist would disengage from the individual 'Paste' & 'Never' in our lifetime, you know that, don't you, boys?" [31]—and on the other by a near-sighted faith in personal contact. "You can't alter people, Ronnie. You can only give them some love and hope they'll take it." [56] Both attitudes preclude any public gesture of action *now*.

Dave and Ada are first seen firmly involved in public action during the Cable Street march, an involvement taken to its extreme in Dave's decision to fight in the Spanish Civil War. By act two, both have withdrawn from public action, though not quite in the same manner as Harry. Ada and, from what she says, Dave too, have lost the will to give love to people as well as the will to alter them: "I'm not so sure that I love them enough to *want* to organise them." [41] Charity begins at home, and Ada wants to put herself in order first. She explains: "How can we care for a world outside ourselves when the world inside is in disorder?" [42] It is not necessarily "love" or even respect for those who are or are not to be helped to a better society that Ada would have to feel, but merely some or any kind of value in them. "Oh yes! the service killed any illusions Dave may have once had about the splendid and heroic working class." [41] As this remark of Ada's suggests, the couple set out with expectations pitched too high, and in reaction have surpassed Harry's perhaps indifferent tolerance.

For Ada and Ronnie, the excess of the expectations and the depth of the fall are partly Sarah's responsibility. General benevolence is the groundwork of her beliefs: "Love comes now. You have to start with love. How can you talk about socialism otherwise?" [28] Ada, unable to emulate this, finds it overpowering. "What audacity," she protests, "tells you you can harbour a billion people in a theory?" [42–3] Ronnie too at last returns home to confess that he has been unable to imitate in practice or even accept in theory Sarah's evaluation of the unregenerate masses.

SARAH: What does it matter if your father was a weakling, or the man you worked with was an imbecile. They're human beings.

RONNIE: That doesn't mean a thing. [76]

Like Ada and Harry he finds his mother's energetic benevolence impossible and meaningless. He faces the final curtain as much appalled as unconvinced by Sarah's demands.

Among the minor characters, disillusionment leads to a reaction not dissimilar to Ada's in effect, but impelled by different fallibilities. As Ada had found the principle sound but the human material corrupt, so Monty Blatt shares Sarah's commitment to human warmth and togetherness, but turns his back on plans to stabilise and spread this warmth. "There's nothing more to life than a house, some friends, and a family—take my word." [62] His grasp on the principles was always shaky, as Dave had noticed in act one: "Sometimes, Monty, I think you only enjoy the battle, and that one day you'll forget the ideal." [21] But the others, Prince, Hymie and Cissie, while retaining allegiance to the ideal are also above the actual battle. The pocket of domestic comfort becomes sufficient.

Ada's image of the happiness possible in industrial society as a flower growing in a jungle [42] can be adapted to fit what Monty has found: he accepts the jungle if he can have the flower. Ada rejects the jungle and so rejects its flowers too. Paradoxically, of all these it is Cissie, accused by Sarah of coldness and calculation, who has kept up longest her undemonstrative relations with the remnants of the old circle, as well as her strenuous trade union work—which has retired her before she has grown tired of it.

The characters, then, have run a gamut of social attitudes by the end of the play, a range that their own complexity redeems from the possibilities of seeming merely paradigmatic, whilst the personal interaction within the plot fleshes over the bones of the underlying social patterning. Harry and Sarah's relationship is a crucial demonstration of how psychological conflict mirrors social conflict, in an intimate twofoldness easily missed by the superficial observer, in spite of Sarah's spelling out of the parallel. To return to the analogy between *Chicken Soup* and *Ghosts*, Sarah's intolerance of her husband's fecklessness is as deleterious in effect as Mrs Alving's strong rein on the Captain. The discrepancy between Sarah's general even-temperedness and her recurrent hostility towards Harry's failings can hardly be anything but unfortunate in influencing their children: thus, after Ada's passionate reaction to her parents' quarrel in act one, Ronnie escapes to the washing-up from a family row, and Ada, soon afterwards, to her own home.

Ronnie tacitly reproaches Sarah with this during their final confrontation. "I've got to have light and love," she says. "Ronnie looks up at her meaningfully," Wesker directs, as she goes on: "You think I didn't love your father enough, don't you?" [75] And she describes Harry's crucial —to her—failure towards his family during the slump. On a personal, emotional level this is an adequate and natural explanation. On the level of abstract principle, her reaction has much in common with Dave's rejection of regressive servicemen. The difference is that she does go on fighting and hoping to reclaim Harry, however tactless and self-defeating—"well-meaning but maddening" [12]—her methods may be.

Thematically, Sarah's hostility towards Harry is all one with her antagonism towards the apathy that obstructs the fulfilment of her ideals. In his inertia, evasiveness, and unobtrusive deterioration Harry not only "symbolises" opponents of social happiness such as the inimical "they", but also (his function in the play being quite complex) personifies the system in another way, as its victim—he is both cause and effect, self-perpetuating. This is what Sarah spells out, succinctly but explicitly: "all my life I've fought. With your father and the rotten system that couldn't help him." [75] This is important, indicating how far Wesker has shifted environment (in the widest sense) into the dominating position occupied in Ibsen's works by heredity.

So, although Harry might well have proved too intractable a problem for Sarah even had she employed a more insightful approach, and is said by Cissie to be taking after *his* mother, and although Ronnie points out his own similarities to his father in character as well as appearance, the *possibility* of change is still the vital factor. Another set of conditions, another society, could "alter people" if only by causing a different combination of latent characteristics to surface. Even here, in the event Ronnie is *not* a pre-programmed facsimile of his father—who, as Sarah remarks, "would never have left his mother to go abroad as you did". [76]

Sarah herself, as the standard by which the alienation of the other characters is measured—and especially since stubborn resistance to change is one of her idiosyncratic traits—changes little over the years. But the slight yet telling shift from her original prompt energy to the physically modified weariness that has to be shaken off before the essential fire springs up responsively to Ronnie's challenge, makes for one of the most moving developments in the play. Harry's slow lapse into paralysis keeps pace with the disaffection of the seen and unseen friends of the Kahns' youth. He is brisk in self-defence in act one, eager in reading and more accurately informed than Sarah. Admittedly this interest has a theoretical bias, but it is more than he musters in acts two and three. Evasive towards Sarah's nagging in the first act, when pushed with his back to the wall he participates energetically in the eventual quarrel. At the end of act two he is provoked into an outburst of rage, but this time it is a tantrum of no more than childish proportions, in response to a niggling frustration. A change has taken place, an organic deepening, within the lines of character already drawn. Wesker's sureness of characterisation means that his characters have consistent personalities that do develop in the strictest sense of the word, as we shall see again in *Roots*—they are not twisted by the demands of the plot into making convenient but unconvincing changes of course.

Ada's transformation from the enthusiastic fourteen-year-old who cannot be kept away from the Cable Street barricades to a "weary at soul" twenty-five-year-old is certainly considerable. During the decade-long time-lag between acts one and two she becomes cool, self-contained, reserved, fond of being alone, and fastidious in the standards she requires of other people; but, again, there are intimations of this latent process of change, in the family quarrels she recoils from in both acts. Reaction against home influence is plainly as potent a factor as simple imitation would have been—and perhaps her new self seems less alien within the family when compared with the not dissimilar cool taciturnity of her aunt Cissie.

This is why the functioning of heredity as a factor in Ronnie's loss of his social faith is important: it underpins a major reversal, deepening its nature from that of a possibly temporary depression to that of a potentially permanent embitterment. Between the scenes of act two, Ronnie perhaps loses some singlemindedness, but, still enthusiastic and optimistic, he tells Cissie: "I have all the world at my fingertips. Nothing is mixed up." [48] His brisk energy in the second act is unlike even Harry's brighter self of act one: but as Ronnie crumples into a chair in the final scene of the play, his rhythm of movement has finally come to resemble his father's.

Here, as in the remainder of the Trilogy, Ronnie is peripheral to the dramas of other people, hovering on the edge, observing, involved vicariously, trying to predict his own drama from theirs. His consciously ironic appeal to Sarah is "Do it *for* me." [72] And he had been hurt by Ada's disillusion because he got all his ideas from her and Dave— it is part of his personality to accept others' influence, though his adoption of the ideas is active enough. This malleability reinforces the impression that Ronnie is not strong enough to bear the central weight of the play's theme, which deals with ethics, rather than the nature of knowledge or a conviction or truth.

Ronnie's eventual collapse has such significance not just because he is the long-awaited prodigal, held in reserve for two scenes, whose return has been eagerly anticipated, and not just because the final curtain adds an exclamation mark to an emotional episode, but because his new emptiness is the climax to a prepared and pervasive stressing of apathy and dissociation—the game of solo, then separation, the girl outside screaming for Philip in a travesty of a passionate scene, the mention of a neighbour's suicide. The characters thus caught up in their own anguished decisions, rounded and contradictory as play-analysts feel they have a right to expect, simultaneously carry the currents of a flowing social tide.

Arrested and isolated at any stage of the play, they contrast pointedly in social reactions as well as in private temperaments one with another. Followed continuously through their whole development, they illustrate in themselves the changes of social climate over the pre- and post-war decades—"the" thirties, and "the" forties—without requiring Wesker to deal with the direct impact of public affairs as plot elements. Even the opening Cable Street demonstration is primarily an off-stage dynamo activating the Kahn family, so that their intermingling with the sympathetic crowd of minor characters is the first impression received. In the subsequent acts, the withdrawal of this communal context indirectly reflects the characters' more individual reactions to world events: but such events are not worked directly into the main patterning of plot incidents.

Thus the integration of character and theme in *Chicken Soup* ensures that its basic structure is balanced and strong, and the working out of this in the detailed substance of the action is always consistent and true to its framework, preserving at the same time a diversity and independence about the minutiae. There are faults of construction associated with scene-setting which are recurrent in the other early plays—ranging from Sarah's only slightly unnecessary expansion "Cissie? Harry's sister?" [24] to Ronnie's programme-note "The war's been over a year already. Imagine! I was only nine when he left. . . ." [37] Similarly the argument between Cissie and Sarah fills in background under cover of convincingly commonplace family recrimination until the author betrays an apologetic self-consciousness in Cissie's final "Yes, yes—so I know all this already." [28]

However, explicitness is helpful in the stage directions, which, besides filling in the detail expected in naturalistic drama, justifiably try to prevent too simple interpretations of the dialogue in performance—although it *is* to such simplifications that Wesker's readers and audiences have been all too prone. Even as gentle an authorial hint as the note to Sarah's "well-meaning but maddening attempt to point out to a weak man his weakness" [12] blocks the temptation to label and separately pigeon-hole the pair as "good wife" and "bad husband".

Complexity beneath a veneer of simplicity has made most of Wesker's plays surprisingly cryptic to his audiences—especially to those who fail to notice any internal contradictions. But in *Chicken Soup* it is precisely such a failure to come to terms with complexity, as Sarah has uneasily done, that cuts the ground from under Ronnie's feet. Sarah's complexity also ensures that though she answers and so qualifies Ronnie's pessimism, her age, and the totality of the disillusioned opposition to her among family and friends, modifies the "message" of her optimism: the conclusion is more open than either of the chief protagonists prefers to think.

Diagrammatically, the course of *Chicken Soup with Barley* could be plotted along the horizontal axis of Sarah's steadfastness,[19] the hopeful starts of the other characters along parallel straight lines plummeting downwards as the action proceeds. Such courses plotted for the characters in the second play of the Trilogy, *Roots*, would follow slow but steady downward curves—until the sudden, triumphant upward-soaring of Beatie Bryant at the end of the play's closing act. And maybe it is because this conclusion conceals—though it does *not* in fact eliminate—the ambivalent pessimism of its companion pieces that *Roots* has remained the most popular work of the three, even as an examination set-text. Thus, it is also the only one to have been given a professional London revival, at the Royal Court in February 1967. But it was first performed at the Belgrade, Coventry, in May 1959, that production transferring to the Royal Court in June, to the Duke of York's in the following month, and seen in its proper sequence in the next year's Trilogy season.

Its links with its sibling plays are, however, at first sight rather tenuous. Thus, Beatie Bryant connects up with the Kahns only as the long-standing girl-friend of Ronnie, and hopefully his future wife. Beatie has returned to her native

Norfolk for a few weeks' holiday with her family: and here Ronnie is to join her, and be shown-off. To please him she has imitated or tolerated his political and cultural progressiveness: but it is not until the end of the play, when she suddenly learns by letter that he has left her, that she is shocked into digesting, applying and explicating these opinions herself—thus proving the success of Ronnie's influence over her just as he has chosen to relinquish it. This positive climactic advance naturally comes as a relief and reassurance to an audience. Beatie has risen to her opportunities after all, is saved from the flames, and eclipses the immovable Bryants. But "whatever she will do they will continue to live as before". [151]

Roots and *I'm Talking About Jerusalem* approach the same subject—the comparatively primitive life of a money-starved rural society—from almost opposite formal directions. In both plays the subject is presented in deliberately anti-romantic terms, so as to emphasise how alien the circumstances of twentieth-century agriculturalism are to the world that Dave and Ada Simmonds want to recreate in their rural retreat—the world, say, of George Eliot's *Adam Bede*, with its pastoral dairies and dedicated carpenter-craftsmen. For the social fabric of that England, its economic foundation and its sense of practical and of moral purpose have disappeared. Oddly enough, there is a mention of rootlessness in *Adam Bede*—of Hetty Sorrel, as one of those plants "that have hardly any roots: you may tear them from their native nook of rock or wall, and just lay them over your ornamental flower-pot, and they blossom none the worse".[20]

But the point is precisely that Hetty is, in this respect, an exception, whereas by the mid-nineteen-fifties *all* the farming people in *Roots* have become as loosely attached to what they have to do and to each other as the unfortunate Hetty. All are misfits now, and the play is called *Roots* because its characters have none. The Bryants may well have lived in their East Anglian neighbourhood for generations, but, just as much as the factory workers Dave believes to have been brutalised by monotony, they are dissociated from the system they work for, and unconcerned with movements and advances of value to humanity generally because they know nothing about them. Rather than belonging to a community, the Bryants drift wherever tides beyond their control take them.

In effect, the everyday rhythms of a style of country life which has been streamlined—not necessarily with the aid of machinery but by the expedient of fewer people doing more work—can be quite as numbing, alike in home or farm, as factory work, work in a restaurant kitchen, or any other artificially pressurised routine, whether or not it is concerned with live creatures. The routine contributes to the confusion in the cottage of Beatie's sister, Jenny Beales: her mother, though seeming to rely at least partly on a soft rainwater-tank for water, has power for an electric cooker, but Jenny has neither gas, running water nor electricity. She obviously does not care much about her surroundings: but a stage direction explains that if these are untidy, "it is because there is a child in the house and there are few amenities, so that the mother is too overworked to take much care". [83]

The houseproud sister Susan is evidently better off in various ways, and the television set in her council house is a rare luxury in the neighbourhood. In Mrs Bryant's case, though, a housewife's daytime solitude is aggravated by the isolation of her cottage, helping to narrow her experience and lending an artificial importance to the trivial incidents that do come her way: her mental horizon is limited more by lack of stimulus than by physical fatigue. But Beatie no longer lives or works in these conditions: so her development is to be the test of how permanently constricting the effect of such an environment is.

The conflict in *Roots*, then, is between a life-denying environment, in this case agricultural, and a stimulating one —that is, Beatie's earlier, off-stage life with Ronnie. Harry Kahn's theory from *Chicken Soup*, to be repeated by Ronnie in *I'm Talking About Jerusalem*, is quoted by Beatie here, too: "You can't change people, he say, you can only give them some love and hope they'll take it." [129] This is seen to work once in the trilogy, here in *Roots*, though perhaps it's not at first apparent how marginal in its effect such an approach is doomed to be. Beatie is saved because she happens to have attracted a proselytising thinker into a love affair. How many in need of salvation can hope for that? All learning is easier when the learner feels respect and admiration, and especially love, for a teacher who is also a model: and so Beatie's ulterior motives for pleasing Ronnie do give her a special receptivity, perhaps in spite of herself, towards his ideas. However, the end of the play is a comment on the limits of the effectiveness of this personal, diffusionist approach: the rest of the Bryants are impervious and will continue impervious to change, even though Beatie has gained control of her own arguments.

The "some love" that is all that one individual can offer to another has in fact to be quite a lot of love, if it is to prove powerful enough to raise the enmeshing net of circumstances. A dramatisation of this is Beatie's attempt to hand on what she has learnt to her mother by making her listen to and register the attractions of Bizet's *L'Arlesienne*. She is successful thus far, her enthusiasm and strong personality imposing themselves on her mother, but this one isolated lesson is counterbalanced not only by the Bryants' later discouraging reactions to plot developments, but by what the naturalistic action so insistently affirms—Mrs Bryant's continuing solitude, money worries, uncongenial home life and trivial local intercourse. Mrs Bryant may be rather fond in future of this particular piece of music: but, because so much expenditure of love, care and patience is needed to help one person *begin* to grow, as the main action of *Roots* shows, a little love dabbed on here and there in such episodes naturally has an even more sporadic effect. Ronnie's more extensive experiment in discipleship, and its precarious success in bringing about the growth of one person's mind, supplies *Roots* with its dominant plot-line, and its realisation in Beatie's progress towards articulacy.

Another cause of the play's wide popularity may be the compactness that Beatie's dominance gives to the action, which is close and well-defined in its time-structure. There is no one to rival Beatie in importance as the major character, for the difference in stature between her and the other Bryants is much greater than that between Sarah and her family. And since the action is concerned with this one stage in her life, its unity is more self-evident even than the episodically illustrated problems of Dave and Ada Simmonds in *I'm Talking About Jerusalem*. Moreover, this focusing of attention on a change in Beatie herself from one state to another within a few weeks corresponds in the other two plays to a much more gradual modification of general attitudes—in Sarah's view of the world, or in the crusading zeal of the Simmonds.

Beatie's development thus more or less controls the play's internal structuring. The first act in the Beales' cottage is largely expository in function, though strong in the interest of its local colour. The second act demonstrates Beatie's currently amphibious state between new and old worlds. And both have the kind of localised movement that comes from the slow revelation of a static picture. Then the last act precipitates two brisk reversals into the action—first,

Ronnie's farewell letter, then Beatie's sudden jolt into awareness. The divergence between words and deeds—the irrelevance of Beatie's acquired arguments to her actual behaviour—is carefully illustrated in the first two acts, whereas if we had seen Beatie in London conscientiously (even unsuccessfully) acting up to Ronnie's expectations, this troubling divergence would have been obscured. Here she comments: "Funny that! Soon ever I'm home again I'm like I always was—it don' even seem I bin away." [86]

Nevertheless, Beatie's development is slower than, and by no means as abrupt and disjointed as, the traumatic effect of Ronnie's letter in the last act might imply. For her first-act reversion to an earlier self is not complete, and her state in the first and second acts is, as I have described it, amphibious, divided between natural and acquired standards. Though she automatically starts reading the Beales' comics, she applies Ronnie's arguments pertinently in opposing her brother-in-law Jimmy's opinions on strikers and the territorial army, and in pinpointing the incongruity of her mother's life:

> God in heaven Mother, you live in the country but you got no—no—no majesty. You spend your time among green fields, you grow flowers and you breathe fresh air and you got no majesty. Your mind's cluttered up with nothing and you shut out the world. [127]

It is important to notice here that Beatie, not being by any means stupid, is quite capable of understanding a short concrete argument, and is particularly quick to observe cause and effect in her own upbringing—those things which immediately and exclusively concern herself—even if she has to feel for Ronnie's idiom in which to express her observation.

But this is another aspect of rootlessness, the myopic sensibility that keenly appreciates what affects itself but cannot relate this—"only connect" it—to wider issues. Beatie therefore sees that her mother's mind is full of nothing and that her own upbringing has been deficient in timely opportunities, but the more theoretical phrases she has acquired, "something about commercial world blunting our responses", [115] fail for her to relate to what she sees or the way she sees it. Thus, it is the integrated, comprehended connection she learns to make between theory and experience, not the ability to string the old phrases together in better order, that is Beatie's crucial achievement at the final curtain.

When Ronnie's letter breaks off their relationship, Beatie's recognition of how she has proved inadequate is far from sudden, though the importance to her of this inadequacy has previously been obscured. Although she has duly relayed her acquired opinions, she has never wholly *believed* she believes in them. After annoying Jimmy by talking him into a corner, she admits that her superiority is illusory because she can only call on it at intervals—a sense of superiority is no part of her everyday life with Ronnie's friends:

Because I'm stubborn, I'm like Mother, I'm stubborn. Somehow I just can't bring myself to ask, and you know what? I go mad when I listen to them . . . Sometimes I don't say anything, sometimes I go to bed or leave the room. Like Jimmy—just like Jimmy. [93]

And after trying to teach her mother how to criticise a pop long, Beatie has to stop because she knows she has not grasped the rationale justifying the critical phrases, and she is dimly aware that this is cause for uneasiness: "I'm worried about Ronnie I suppose. I have that same row with him. I ask him exactly the same questions—what make a pop song third-rate. And he answer and I don't know what he talk about. . . . I don't know what questions to ask or *how* to talk." [115]

Understanding what is demonstrable about Ronnie's ideas without grasping rationally or emotionally their basis in principle is, then, Beatie's rootlessness. And she does not deceive herself about the value she puts on these ideas:

> He was interested in all the things I never even thought about. . . . So I pretended I was interested—but I didn't understand much. All the time he's trying to teach me but I can't take it Jenny. And yet, at the same time, I want to show I'm willing. [94]

Her willingness is rather that of the women's magazine strategist advising how-to-get-your-man by "sharing his interests", than of the earnest culture-starved waif. "Oh don't you worry gal," she tells Jenny,

> it'll be all right once we're married. Once we're married and I got babies I won't need to be interested in half the things I got to be interested in now. [95]

She accepts these, in short, because it pleases Ronnie, not because they are worthwhile or interesting or true.

But at the same time the audience should be able to see that Beatie *has* been affected, if only a little, by experiences that eclipse what had satisfied her before—the sharing of interests may have begun as Ronnie-bait, but has been found quite simply good. After protesting that she "can't take it", she admits, "I couldn't have any other life now." [94] So she is poised rather unhappily between the old life which, comics or no comics, isn't any longer sufficient, and the new, which at once challenges and exasperates her. In the event, Ronnie turns out to have been wiser in telling her, "Give yourself time woman. . . . Time! You can't learn how to live overnight," [115] than in giving her up after three years, which is a short enough "time" in which to undermine a contrary conditioning of nineteen. One remembers the courtier who to please his mistress had to scale peaks of cultural achievement: living up to Ronnie seems more of a crash course in culture than a liberal education.

As in *Chicken Soup*, Ronnie's intervention, this time by letter, provokes the play's dramatic closing speech. In a way, the letter's ostensible information, that Ronnie and Beatie's affair is over, is something of a red herring, because it is Beatie's long speech, "articulate at last", that is the climax of the play, not her first emotional reaction to being jilted. The letter is the catalyst to Beatie's growth, the emotional trigger of an intellectual advance. She begins with deflated self-examination, and for once catches a glimpse of her own idea-less state—as that of a gross, merely absorbing animal (like the wife described by Libby Dobson in *Jerusalem*), the object of Ronnie's terrified accusation: "you don't know who I am or what I'm trying to say—and you don't care do you?" [145]

But then she is brought over the threshold of a distinct new area of articulacy and understanding by her *reasoning* about what she has always recognised clearly, her own and her family's faults: now, the usual sharp recognition is pushed one step further, so that she can "place" these faults, *connect* them with the wider scheme of things—a connection of the kind that has eluded her before, in this case, between her family's life and the commercial interests that exploit the temptations of actual and spiritual laziness. Suddenly things hang together; things connect; things have roots.

Articulacy insistently forces itself on our attention in

Roots. However, the true articulacy attained by Beatie, it must be realised, comprehends both speech and understanding. Her natural liveliness ("Thank God you come home sometimes gal—you do bring a little life with you anyway," [116] as Mrs Bryant puts it) has not only disposed her to pursue Ronnie energetically and to make a trial of his doctrines of living life to the full, but also distinguishes her from her family, its prevailing taciturnity interspersed with sporadic gossiping. This liveliness is not only acted out—to the monotonous pace of the Beales' life, "Beatie's bursts are the exception" [90]—but also appears in her flow of talk once she gets into her stride.

Jimmy and Jenny always understate, which even in handing-on local scandal seems to hint at a fear of words, whereas Mrs Bryant's talk is mainly repetition, and Mr Bryant "don't say too much when he's home". [133] Beatie, too, was once as inarticulate as her fellow-workers when faced by a sheet of blank writing paper: "We couldn't find words." [128] But she has found words, though these may be borrowed from Ronnie, and she uses them: her family's boredom or hostility at the end of the third act has been provoked by Beatie's tendency to demand more of them than conventional questions and comments, jokes and gossip. Articulacy as a concomitant of liveliness and friendliness is not rare, and Mrs Bryant's repetitive gossip under pressure, showing a need to speak but not a need to communicate, intimates how a chattier family could conceal under the noise of simultaneous monologues a real lack of communication. This failure of communication has been a common enough subject of twentieth-century drama: but Beatie's problem is different, because for her the chasm lies between what she knows and what she says, not between what she says and who she speaks to.

In a way Beatie is preparing herself, all the time she stays with her family, to grasp what talking means to Ronnie: to him—because he does, of course, already integrate theory and expression—communication is the important aspect of speech. Seeing words as bridges [88] implies faith in the possibility of contact. Now this faith Beatie already shares, even if she does not realise it, and her communication problems, though *resulting* in hostility or silence, are entirely due to her intellectual difficulties and not to introversion or indifference. In her earnest reproduction of half-understood doctrines she shows how fervently she wants to share what she has acquired with her family—she could much more easily have put on an air of superiority by assuming from the beginning the "oh, what's the use" attitude that comes over her briefly just before she attains articulacy. [147]

By contrast, in the rest of her family alienation is signified by silence. "Susie won't talk to Mother." [133] The elder Bryants quarrel by not speaking, except through Beatie as intermediary, in act one, scene two, whilst the daughter-in-law Pearl and Mrs Bryant "don't talk to each other", [97] and the latter "hevn't spoke to her own mother for three years". [133] Beatie is different from them: she is immediately upset by her father's enforced change of job, and wants to *talk* about it—spontaneously, not because this accords with Ronnie's theories.

Thus, it has to be recognised, in fairness to the truth of the play and the consistency of its characterisation, that Beatie is not a complacent parrot transformed into a human being just in time for the final curtain. In short, her liveliness and her "going up and down in her spirits" [115] are the signs of an essential responsiveness. Her articulacy is already more advanced than her family's, and all the basically communicative showing-off about Ronnie's new ideas makes her more nearly akin to the Kahns than to the other Bryants.

Although the residual Bryants tend to be lumped together

C

in stage directions—"there is no sign of intense living from any of the characters", [90] and "they will continue to live as before" [151]—they are differentiated enough among themselves for Beatie to find a place at one end of a scale of willingness-to-communicate. The unseen sister Susan is perhaps the non-participant *par excellence*, but Beales and Bryants are variegated from the abrupt father Bryant to the facetious Frankie. Jenny, though wrapped up in her house-work, is more perceptive than the others in guessing at the flaws in Beatie's relationship with Ronnie. As much by temperament as through fatigue, however, she is acquiescent in the conditions of her own life.

It is left to the decrepit old non-Bryant, Stan Mann, staggering around the countryside with figurative vineleaves in his hair and alcohol fumes befuddling his brain, to represent the intense life as a rather perverse individualist lives it: and this life is a last flicker before the ambulance picks him up. His regrets for the past and contempt for the present make him a man who for once thrives or throve in his particular environment. "I hed my day. An' I'd do it all the same again. . . ." But "None o' them young 'uns'll do it, hell if they will. There ent much life in the young 'uns." [106] An audience tends, because of his retrospection, to get the impression that he is a genuine old-style country-man, product of some richer rural past, and driven to find a sort of solace in the present.

Thus, his memories relate to the theme of the "commercial world blunting our responses", referring back to a period before the mass media infiltrated the whole community. He has experienced what has been lost by the present younger generation:

None o' them young 'uns'll do it, hell if they will. There ent much life in the young 'uns. Bunch o' weak-kneed

ruffians. None on 'em like livin' look, none on 'em!
You read in them ole papers what go on look, an' you
wonder if they can see. You do! Wonder if they got eyes to
look around them. Think they know where they live?
Course they don't, they don't you know, not one. Blust!
the winter go an' the spring come on after an' they don't
see buds an' they don't smell no breeze an' they don't see
gals, an' when they see gals they don't know whatta do
wi' 'em. They don't! [106]

On the other hand, a character and a speech like this combine to indicate what the play's unity of action may conceal:
for communication, whether commercial or personal, is
only one of the troubles of the characters. Freedom from
conditioning to the third rate would make very little practical
difference to Jenny Beale's life, for example, or to the organisation of Hall Farm. A return to first-hand living, as it was
perhaps experienced in Stan's youth, does no more than
suggest a preferable starting point for the revaluation of all
aspects of society—it does not represent *in itself* a comparative golden age.

Of course, Wesker is under no obligation to offer such an
ideal alternative to the way of life in *Roots* at all. But,
dramatically, what is dubious about Stan Mann and his
picture of the past is that they falsely *seem* to be offering an
ideal—which is not only a questionable one in absolute
terms, but, in aspiring to be a total solution though in fact
answering only one problem, and ignoring, say, economic
and amenity problems, tends to unbalance the dialectical
structure of the play.

Stan's individuality is contained as much in the style of
his dialogue as in what he talks about. The heavy punctua-
tion between items in his back-tracking, accumulative
idiom shows that he is meant to talk more slowly than the

younger characters. The regular emphases in the long speech quoted above—"none on 'em", "You do!", "They don't you know, not one", and the series of "an' they don'ts" —are not repetitions of whole ideas or anecdotes such as betray Mrs Bryant's narrow experience, but make up the rhythm of his individualised eloquence. This exchange, too —about auction sales—suggests the consolidating, developing rhythm by which his conversation proceeds:

> MRS BRYANT: You still visit them things then?
> STAN: Yearp. Pass the ole time away. Pass the ole time.
> MRS BRYANT: Time drag heavy then?
> STAN: Yearp. Time drag heavy. She do that. Time drag so slow, I get to thinkin' it's Monday when it's still Sunday. Still, I had my day gal I say. Yearp. I had that all right. [106]

The Bryants' style of speech is similar but not as ruminative as Stan's. Jenny's repetitions are quicker, running on without such heavy division, and her way of making a point is to say:

> Thaas true Beatie. They're such sods, honest to God they are. Every time there's bin a rise someone get sacked. Without fail. You watch it—you ask father Bryant when you get home, ask him who's bin sacked since the rise. [91]

Or, again: "Many's the time I'd've willingly strangled you— with no prayers—there you are, no prayers whatsoever. Strangled you till you was dead." [98] And part of an oft-repeated story of Mrs Bryant's runs:

> She was standin' in a tub o' water up to her neck. She was!

Up to her neck. An' her eyes had that glazed, wonderin'
look and she stared straight at me she did. Straight at me.
Well, do you know what? I was struck *dumb*. I was *struck
dumb wi'* shock. [126]

Telling the same story over and over, especially in the same
words, saves making the effort of thinking afresh, but these
longer repetitions, like the shorter ones, also show an ear for
a pleasing rhythm which once found is retained, as in Mrs
Bryant's diagnosis of Jimmy's back pains, three times
retailed with the same phrasing.

For the purposes of the play, this dialogue is a good
vehicle for an actor's Norfolk accent. But a tape transcription
of any dialect—of any "real life" speech—would make a
surprising and probably unusable text, and whilst therefore
Wesker can and does only indicate general pronunciation,
it is this basic rhythm in the word and phrase order, not his
"hevs" and "yearps", which gives the dialect authority and
conviction.[21] Oddly enough, the one faltering in style comes
in Ronnie's letter. [144] Unless one accepts as excuse the
hypothesis that embarrassment is making him unusually
stilted, the writer of the letter seems much limper, more
precious and self-conscious, than the energetic, rhetorical,
even explosive speaker we have known—as much in Beatie's
enacted imitations of him as in *Chicken Soup*. The "reasonable" opening ("it wouldn't really work would it?") the
indecisive qualifications ("quite", "really", "pretty"), and
the uneasy forestalling of guilt by self-accusation, add up to
an evasive statement of a case that carries neither a sense of
conviction nor of inspiration, lacking alike the force of
Ronnie's previously retold tirades and the economy of the
Bryants' reticence.

The family's humour is individualised not just because it
is scripted in dialect-style orthography, but because it is

shaped by this normal reticence. A stage direction points out that, in spite of apparent sleepiness, their "sense of humour is keen and dry". [90] Sometimes it is unconscious, as in the automatic and unvarying litany made out of Mrs Bryant's back-to-front indigestion diagnosis, or in Beatie's "I don't quote all the time, I just tell you what Ronnie say." [140] But the characters usually slip a deadpan, understated humour quite intentionally into their exchanges. Thus, the logical follow-up to the slogan about vanilla ice cream coming from the white milk of a Jersey cow is that strawberry ices come from the pink milk of a pink cow. [89] And Mrs Bryant will object to being asked whether the lyric of a pop song makes her "feel better" with "Blust gal! That ent meant to be a laxative!" [114] Quite apart from its rustic accents, this humour is different *in kind* from the histrionic, audience-conscious type approved by the Kahn family.

A certain verbal awkwardness in Wesker's earlier plays, usually unimportant when it comes to staging, is often connected with difficulties of exposition—a pitfall in most naturalistic and quasi-naturalistic plays. But in this, the most purposefully naturalistic play of the trilogy, the difficulties are resolved with great smoothness. Beatie's arrival for an apparently rare visit nicely cues-in news and gossip; the renewed questions about the father of Jenny's illegitimate child and their bafflement are as informative about the speakers as about the subject; and elliptic childhood reminiscences block in the background.

Beatie's recollections of the course of the relationship with Ronnie share another kind of significance. The narrative opening ("From the first day I went to work as waitress in the Dell Hotel . . .") and the argumentative conclusion of her chief retrospective speech are conversational enough: but from the rueful self-assessment with its repetition "and I thought it was easy. I thought everything was easy," the lucid sentences of her narrative unfold more meditatively and tenderly. The emphatic repetitions of her family become the varied, refrain-like echoings of "and I told him no different . . . and I didn't tell him no different", weighted with understated significance. [93–4] Beatie does realise the complications of feelings that her simple sentences nevertheless imply. Simplicity does not reflect obtuseness, and her perceptive unease is a further reason not to underestimate from the first her ability to change. This set-speech of Beatie's shifts away from the naturalism of the interchanging dialogue into the sphere of Beatie's thoughts and back again—and the transitions are as faultlessly managed as the expository content.

Less tactful is the didactic episode of Mrs Bryant's musical education—didactic not so much in that Beatie is literally teaching her mother, as in the feeling that the lesson is really directed in exemplary fashion at the audience. The relation of this kind of episode to the full-scale work of education is touched on above: and, purely within the context of the play, this episode stands out as a superfluous and incongruous simplification of what the rest of the action embodies with greater consistency and sophistication. There is a similarly over-convenient point-making about Stan Mann's sudden, explicit analysis of exploitation: "Them young 'uns is all right though. Long as they don't let no-one fool them, long as they think it out theirselves." [107]

And then there's the heavily ironic juxtaposition in this exchange:

MRS BRYANT: The Union magazine's come.
MR BRYANT: I don't want that ole thing.
BEATIE: Why can't you do something to stop the sackings?
MR BRYANT: You can't, you can't—that's what I say, you can't. Sharp as a pig's scream they are—you just *can't* do nothin'. [120]

However, apart from the conventional act-and-scene frame-work imposed on the action, *Roots* usually avoids ostentatious dramatic effects in the interests of its predominantly natural-istic atmosphere. As with the use of true-to-life dialogue, the presence of dramatic shaping is not optional but a matter of degree, and this shaping dictates such emphases as the curtain-underlining of Beatie's dance in act two and of her long speech in act three.

But, especially in the first two acts, an important aim of the play is to build up a picture of the normal everyday life of the Beales and Bryants—in fact, of the routine in which Beatie was once caught up—not just to record the interesting dramatic conflicts sparked off by Beatie's new ideas. This is the point of the leisurely enactment of certain static episodes, like Jenny's quiet washing-up—"a silence that needs organising" [90]—or Beatie's bath, or the silence of the assembled Bryants, which "is not an awkward silence, just a conversationless room".[22] [137] As an early stage direction states, "the silences are important—as important as the way they speak, if we are to know them". [90-1]

Much of *Roots* is concerned with showing this unspectacu-lar life directly—not pruning away undramatic sequences, still less representing the routine symbolically, as in *The Four Seasons*, or encapsulating the required impression at second-hand in some character's description. So, although there are obviously many plays of greater documentary realism, offering a slice of life with less form and less plot content, *Roots* definitely belongs in the mainstream of their tradition, along with, for example, Hauptmann's *Before Sunrise* and D. H. Lawrence's *The Daughter-in-Law*. For here documented naturalism is not one among many possible production styles, but one that is essential to the play's manner and meaning.

I'm Talking About Jerusalem, the final play in the Trilogy

—first produced in April 1960 at the Belgrade Theatre, Coventry, and then performed in July at the Royal Court in repertory with the others in the sequence—is closer to *Chicken Soup* than to *Roots*, both in its choice of characters and in its extended time-scale. Yet the intermediate work is a helpful introduction to it, setting the East Anglian scene into which Dave and Ada Simmonds arrive as strangers and from which they depart disenchanted, as well as suggesting that silence can be as potent and meaningful a mode of communication as words. For the compulsively-talking Kahns of *Chicken Soup*, silence is the exception: for the hearth-bound Bryants of *Roots* it had been the general rule.

Dave and Ada Simmonds are at the centre of *Jerusalem* as firmly as Ada's mother, Sarah, is at the centre of *Chicken Soup*. Obviously, the couple's continuous presence on stage, their comparative isolation, and the mainly sporadic intrusions of the other characters preclude the rest of the cast from claiming the audience's interest as Ronnie did in the earlier play. Besides this, not only are Dave and Ada themselves positive characters, but the action of the play does not simply happen *to* them, it depends *on* them: it is the result of special activity and unusual determination on their part. Their uncompromising individuality is as effective as the remoteness of their home in thus focusing attention.

I'm Talking About Jerusalem is concerned with the way of life Dave and Ada try to build together in Norfolk. Despairing of the reform of society that had driven Dave to fight in Spain, they reject the industrial rat-race to live out the reformed life themselves, in the country—where Dave can set up a carpenter's shop beside his cottage. The opposition they meet from friends, and even from Dave's own apprentice, wears them down, until finally, craft carpentry unable to co-exist with the products tailored to the mass market, they are forced to return to London. Throughout this play—and in contrast with Sarah, who, though the only exemplar of communism left at the end of *Chicken Soup*, was still part of an organised mass movement—Dave and Ada are alone and unsupported, sole participants in their particular social experiment.

Underlying the surface detail of tilly-lamps and sitting-down chairs, [193] the motive-force of the play—what actually determines the Simmonds' flight from the city—is a revulsion against industrialism: a conflict between a commercial socio-economic system and the traditional ideal of man's individual fulfilment, in harmony with his work, leisure and environment. As a practical problem this ranks with the moral dilemma Beatie posed in *Roots*: the Simmonds' solution is to make at least their own lives consistent with their ideal. One important effect is that the progress of the play by tension and conflict reflects the hostile, defensive attitude implicit in this working-out of salvation. Dave and Ada's struggle is different from Sarah's because it is a fight against, not for, society.

Looking for a moment at the Trilogy as a whole, one notices a slight shift in the Simmonds' attitude between the first and third plays: in *Chicken Soup* the negative side of their retreat is exemplified in a revulsion against the unregenerate proletariat—"lipsticked, giggling morons" and men "like animals". [41] In *Jerusalem* there is less condemnation of the morons and animals themselves, while most of the rancour is reserved for the society of which they are the end products. The shift by omission is slight: but it is significant, because an emphasis on society's responsibilities relates closely to the question of environment, one of the key themes of Wesker's work.

In the first part of the Trilogy, Ada had said that "the only rotten society is an industrial society. It makes a man stand on his head and then convinces him he is good-looking."

[42] And she described that society as a jungle. Here (from time to time) Dave and Ada are more explicit: industrial society or "the city", now conceived as a Cobbettian wen, needs destroying not primarily because of its aesthetic failings, "smoke and petrol fumes" and all, but because of its effect on its inhabitants, who are brutalised.

> All their humanity gone! These you call men? All their lives they're going to drain their energy into something that will give them nothing in return. [167]

And so the Simmonds are trying to ignore these social pressures and live in a human way "on an individual level", [185] as they might if the rest of society did the same.

However, their severance from the rest of the world is not and cannot be total. Dave's indignant indictment *is* equivalent to Sarah's militancy in this, that it shows more concern than the apathetic majority's indifferent tolerance. The Simmonds have "left communism behind", [165] and their ideal is traditionally socialist: as Dave puts it, "Nothing's wrong with socialism Sarah, only we want to live it—not talk about it." [166] Ada complains that "All anyone talks about is taking over capitalist society, but no one talks about really changing it," and Dave's explicit rejoinder is "No of course we can't change it" [167]—just as Ada later echoes, "But God forbid we should ever imagine that we're changing that world by living here." [185] The dehumanising effects of society can only be mitigated so far as they themselves are concerned. Yet, in Dave's final apologia, the suggestion is that he *was* expecting some kind of response from commercial society: "Face it—as an essential member of society I don't really count. . . . Here I've been, comrade citizen, presenting my offerings and the world's rejected them. . . . Maybe Sarah's right, maybe you can't build on your own." [221–2]

He has been disappointed in—what? The Simmonds' experiment has not been by any means a simple self-indulgence. It has been lived according to a firmly-held principle, and was to have been the living proof of that principle's viability. To Ronnie the experiment justified socialism and showed its governmental failures to be incidental not inevitable: "Well, thank God, I thought, it works!" But Sarah mocks him: "Did you expect the world to suddenly focus on them and say 'Ah, socialism is beautiful,' did you, silly boy?" [220] To some extent this is what Dave and Ada, as well as Ronnie, *have* hoped, in spite of their disclaimers: that "the world" would recognise that Jerusalem could be built by a carpenter. Dave sees himself not as a one-man revolution but as a voice crying in what Sarah certainly considers a wilderness. To be precise, the Simmonds' practical experiment is to live out an active testimony—"*not* words. At last something more than just words." [167] It is in this sense that Dave is a prophet—paradoxically yet truly a spokesman for his own Jerusalem.

I'm Talking About Jerusalem, like *Roots* and *Their Very Own and Golden City* in varying degrees, is an ironic title. Jerusalem does not materialise, and "talking" is what Dave and Ada shun obsessively as, over and over again, they complain of the difficulties and failures of verbal communication. This distrust of words is, it should be stressed, a particular trait of the Simmonds' characters, not a commonplace dramatising of the "failure of communication" theme. Similarly, it is a trait specifically of Ronnie's character that he has been reduced from his concept of words as bridges in *Roots* to a depressed belief in Pirandellian mental fluidity here. "As soon as I say something, somehow I don't believe it." [218] Dave is tired of the impotence that seems to be the corollary of copious debating and he reacts particularly against the Kahn family's compulsive loquacity: "I talked enough! You bloody Kahns you! You all talk. Sarah, Ronnie, all of you. I talked enough! I wanted to do something." [211] On the other hand Ada, unlike the other Kahns, is temperamentally opposed to discussion: she is occasionally angered into outbursts, but quickly withdraws, and if not thus provoked does not easily find words for her more personal feelings.

The Simmonds' testimony is unobtrusive because it substitutes deeds for the suspect words, and so the other characters find it hard to extract from them anything that sounds like a manifesto. Ronnie wants the world to know his sister's solution, but Dave is unco-operative—"I'm not going to make speeches, Ronnie" [165]—and when a misunderstanding arises Ada wants to abandon explanations, to Sarah's annoyance. Such a refusal to rationalise inadequately in words is consistent with this dour, isolated experiment within a hostile society, whereas verbal communication is obviously essential to Sarah's communal, aggregative vision of socialism. And so she reprimands her daughter:

SARAH: Ada stop it! Stop it! Impatience! What's the matter with you all of a sudden. Don't explain! Nothing she wants to explain. No more talking. Just a cold, English you-go-your-way-and-I'll-go-mine! Why?
ADA: Because language isn't any use! Because we talk about one thing and you hear another that's why. [166]

No more talking: but for Ada, this taciturnity is later translated into guilt, when her sick father accuses her—"You hate me and you've always hated me" [198]—not because his accusation is true, but because she has probably given him this impression by her undemonstrative behaviour.

The clearest contrast on this theme in the play is between Ada's confessions:

Perhaps I didn't tell him I loved him. Useless bloody things words are. Ronnie and his bridges. . . . Wait till he's older and he learns about silences—they span worlds. [199]

and Esther Kahn's experience of words as a proof of love:

My mother loved her children. You know how I know? The way she used to cook our food. With songs. She used to hum and feed us. Sing and dress us. Coo and scold us. You could tell she loved us from the way she did things for us. You want to be a craftsman? Love us. You want to give us beautiful things? Talk to us. You think Cissie and I fight? You're wrong silly boy. She talks to me. [211]

In one sense, *Jerusalem* is complementary to *Chicken Soup*: its structural pattern is similar, but the colours of the pattern are reversed. Dave and Ada are at the centre of their play, but their relationship with the other characters, as this refusal to communicate suggests, is generally a warding-off, as compared with Sarah's need to draw-in. *Chicken Soup* begins with a euphoric togetherness, from which most of the characters fall away, leaving Sarah at the end actually and morally alone: but *Jerusalem* begins with the Simmonds' departure from family, old ties, discarded commitments, and ends with their return, after a period of solitude, to a life more comprehensible to those friends and relations they had left.

Once more Ronnie's moral dependence on the central characters adds a further dimension to the theme which catches them up: his direct action, enthusiasms and failures are quite different from the Simmonds' isolated primitivism, but depend on the same inspiration. As long as the socialist ideal works in controlled conditions, it seems worth Ronnie's while to struggle with intractable human material, backed up as he is by this proven viability of his vision. In defiance of the Simmonds' wish to prove their principles only for themselves, Ronnie sees them as a significant test case. "The world—will watch you," [167] he warns, and with the couple's return to London his moral anchor gives way too: "I used to watch you and boast about you. Well, thank God, I thought, it works! But look at us now, now it's all of us." [220]

Paradoxically, in spite of Dave's belief that "visions don't work", [222] it is thus his own practice that has been Ronnie's vision. And when he says that "anyone would think it's your experiment that failed, you with your long face", Ronnie's reply is only half melodramatic: "O my God, how near the knuckle that is." [218] His despair at one moment, and wish to persist longer in the doomed experiment at another, are the alternatives that throw into relief the Simmonds' characteristically dogged picking up of pieces and starting afresh. Yet the final exchanges between Ronnie and Sarah show him too moving away from despair towards recovery: "We must be bloody mad to cry," [224] he shouts defiantly, and indeed to cry here would not be to care in the way that brings life.

But that last exchange does not upset the balance of the play—for in that balance Ronnie carries relatively little weight.[23] *Jerusalem* is episodic, but it covers less time than *Chicken Soup*, moving from 1946 in the first scene to 1959 in the last. Ronnie and Sarah appear in these opening and closing episodes, the moving-in and the moving-out, and in between various peripheral characters appear to confront the Simmonds—all of these, except Ronnie and Aunt Cissie, seeking, sometimes from the kindest motives, to undermine their inspiration. Sarah's and Esther's objections are similar in kind. In the first scene Sarah asks: "What's socialism without human beings tell me?" [166] and (a stage direction underlining this as "the real question") "What's wrong with socialism that you have to run to an ivory tower?" [166] At the end she remarks to Ronnie, "I'm always telling you you can't change the world on your own—only no one listens to me." [216] Changing the world is an ambition Dave and Ada always deny, but Dave has earlier quoted a variant—"Maybe Sarah's right, maybe you can't build on your own"—which is, indeed, the "real question" in the play. [222]

More emotionally and less theoretically Aunt Esther complains that Dave and Ada won't discuss their troubles any more, Dave's confirmatory rejoinder being "We're tired Esther, leave us alone, yes?" [210] But she says: "You want to build Jerusalem? Build it! Only maybe we wanted to share it with you." [213] To be fair, though, if Esther keeps telling Dave and Ada they are mad to persist, she can hardly expect to be accounted a fellow-traveller along their road. However, at the root of her own and Sarah's opposition is incomprehension, and this again has to be put down to lack of communication. Neither the principles of the experiment are understood nor the nature of the Simmonds' personal need to live it out—and so neither intellectual nor uncritical emotional support can be sustained.

Libby Dobson, Dave's old army friend, contributes an attack from the theoretical side, his hostility and disillusionment weighing more with Dave because of his earlier friendship. Libby used to stand to him in the position that Dave still stands to Ronnie, and Ronnie's later sense of betrayal at the moving out is similar to Dave's feeling of betrayal by his former comrade and mentor. Yet, inasmuch as Libby's reasons for cynicism are based on his particular and individual circumstances—his wives, his renegade garage partners—they are not conclusive (this is a point made explicitly in that much later play, *The Friends*): in proof of which we see Dave ultimately reacting differently to his own failure. Apart from his personal bitterness, however, Libby has pertinent objections to offer which are apparently unanswerable—which remain, at least, unanswered.

These objections firstly cast doubt upon the Simmonds' independence of the society they have rejected. When Ada repeats to Libby their well-worn protest that they have no ideas about changing the world, he asks: "Then there's not much point doing this sort of thing, is there?" [185] And he accuses them with some justice of dilettantism.

> . . . *that's* the logical conclusion. If no man should be tied to turning out screws all his life, then that's what it means. . . . No humdrum jobs, then no anything. [186]

This is true, and Dave is evading the point when he disclaims the exclusive aim of propagating happiness: for even the tilly-lamp user is profiting by there being a tilly-lamp component maker at routine work somewhere. Unless every object the Simmonds use from cold water pipes to wine-bottles is a handmade artefact, they are condoning not condemning, and participating in rather than rejecting the workings of capitalist society.

The illusory nature of their independence is dramatised less explicitly by the remaining characters, Colonel Dewhurst and Sammy, and by off-stage agents such as the abortive customer Selby, the lorry-driver who damages Dave's furniture by his thoughtlessness, and, appropriately, the bank manager. According to Dave's classification of their opponents into "the cynics, the locals, the family", [212] the Colonel belongs with Sammy among the locals, particularly as both embody the influence of society economically rather than personally. He influences the action when Dave steals some unwanted rolls of lino, flusters himself into denying it, and is dismissed by the Colonel, for whom he has been working while saving to start his carpenter's shop.

On the simplest level this deliberately ambiguous episode shows that Dave as an employee is as dependent as any factory-slave. More important, his character is shown here in a less than favourable light, and the temptation to see him as an austere patriarch is not so strong. Ada calls his stealing one of the "habits of factory life", [192] and it is, indeed, reminiscent of the kitchen staff's "perquisites", and of Harry Kahn's nightly handful of jelly-babies from the sweet factory. However, more emotional weight and effect is attached to this episode than its theatrical significance can justify: the theft of the lino does not seem relevant enough to the main theme to be given the prominence it dramatically demands in a play that is otherwise relatively uneventful in the strict sense.

The role of Sammy the apprentice is more straightforward. His relationship with Dave is ethically admirable and quite unlike Dave's with the Colonel, but Dave's attempts to proselytise are more than counterbalanced by the conventional social values—money, getting on—that press upon Sammy from other quarters. Then, of course, Dave's carpentry trade has to reach some sort of compromise with the commercial system if he is to make a living from it. His products are competing with mass-produced furniture, and this affects how he works in various ways: his customers' expectations are geared to mass-produced values, and the ethos of the careless lorry-driver forces Dave to give up the prized barn workshop within view of his house. Because the aims and standards of the people on whom his living depends are different from his, without malice they act in a way that is incompatible with his survival.

The lesson that has been learnt by the final curtain is that even "on an individual level", an idealistic life is affected by the non-idealistic society that environs it. This lesson is exemplified in the series of confrontations with the various outsiders, which forms the substance of the play; and by its close the Simmonds' experiment has failed. I call it a lesson but, as so often in Wesker's work, the significance of the incidents is so obliquely presented that the audience may be forgiven for leaving with the "message" that the socialist vision is utopian and unworkable.

Episodic in form, the confrontations in the play share a common purpose: and an audience's reaction to Dave's complaint of opposition from cynics, locals and family should not simply be pity for the Simmonds' bad luck. Their activities, their rationale, their attitude that half *invites* opposition, can be traced back to the deepest lines of their personalities. Sarah and Esther observe that both Dave and (especially) Ada have changed and become more reserved and uncommunicative. When Libby Dobson asks whether they have taken their theory to its logical conclusions, the answer is no—because their position depends heavily on their *temperamental* need to shun a world they despise. Their *emotional* reactions have shaped their course according to the most compatible political principle.

Sarah's theoretic position is no less built on a particular emotional bent of character, but her fellow-feeling is an acknowledged basis of her beliefs. *Jerusalem* is a study of two complex characters whose complexities manifest yet disguise themselves in the taking of apparently objective decisions. The Simmonds do not realise themselves how much of their inspiration is emotional, and the result is some confusion in explaining their motives, and some blind spots in planning their movements.

The characterisation, then, interacts organically with the

more abstract level of the play. Ada, paradoxically, is quite articulate about her inarticulacy. "Everybody says I'm cold and hard," she remarks. "People want you to cry and gush over them." [199] She will only give rein to her feelings in privacy, but the silence she imposes on herself is involuntary. "Do you think I know why I behave the way I behave?" she asks: [199] but this bewilderment does not imply that indecisiveness is among the main traits of her character. In persisting with their difficult life, and in being ready to start again when it fails, she is, as she says, like her mother in strength and indomitability at least. "I shall survive every battle that faces me too." [200]

Dave is less introverted and, perhaps because he is seen interacting with more characters by way of business, he appears to expect more of other people. It is he who registers disappointment at his failures of contact, whether with Colonel Dewhurst or with Libby Dobson—and one gets the impression that Ada's steady determination is based not on a Griselda-like sense of patience as a virtue but on her initially more pessimistic expectations.

Though Dave refers generally to opposition from the family, Sarah, Esther and Cissie are very different characters as they are seen in relation to the Simmonds. Esther is full of uncomplicated, spontaneous family affection, whereas Sarah fits even affection into a philosophical frame of reference, whilst Cissie reserves judgement, drily tolerating the discomforts of country life as she had tolerated Harry's decline. Of the outsiders, Colonel Dewhurst nicely exemplifies Wesker's selective use of psychology for his characters, and might helpfully be compared with Osborne's Colonel Redfern in *Look Back in Anger*. For whereas Redfern, like the vanished way of life he remembers, is sympathetic and attractive *in himself*, the main point about Colonel Dewhurst is that, while he is not so dispassionately inhuman as the farm manager in *Roots*, he does have a *non-human* relationship with Dave. His behaviour in dismissing Dave for stealing is natural, far from precipitate, and expresses some kindness, but we see little of the face behind the farmer—which is because of the way dramatic characterisation is being made to function in his case, as in the case of the officers in *Chips with Everything*.

One's readier and deeper understanding of Colonel Redfern was, of course, relevant to certain complexities in the relationship of Jimmy and Alison Porter: but whereas Colonel Dewhurst and his hierarchy are not of intimate, personal significance to Dave and Ada, they are of *practical* significance to the workings of their social pattern. Dewhurst is also important not as an individual but as a contrast to Dave and Sammy. Thus, it is not the Colonel's personality and its accumulative development that matter in the play, but his actions. His reasons for those actions are recognisable but irrelevant.

The pattern of the relationships that interweaves between the characters is as important or more important than the depiction of the characters for their own sake. The Colonel-Dave, Dave-Sammy, and the Libby-Dave, Dave-Ronnie double relationships have been mentioned: and the satisfactory mutual tolerance of Cissie and Esther, which suffuses the latter's speech on talking, is another contrast that contains an implicit comment upon the Simmonds' life. But, especially as the play shows their attempted independence of most social interaction, the central relationship should evidently be that between Dave and Ada.

Citing besides these two such couples as Sarah and Harry or Ronnie and Beatie, Wesker has said of his plays that "in the background was always a concern with the problem of male-female relationships".[24] But in fact the relationship between Dave and Ada is less important in itself than their centrality might suggest, partly because they are exceptional among the couples in being fully agreed on matters of principle, well-matched intellectually, and of varied but compatible temperaments. Problems between them are usually of marginal importance. Consider Ada's comment on Dave's lino contretemps: "By Christ, Dave—your ideals have got some pretty big leaks in places haven't they?" The conclusion is cruelly objective, and a stage direction adds that "Dave is deeply hurt by this and Ada realises she has struck deeply. Perhaps this is the first time she has ever hurt him so deeply." [192–3] That this first time should relate to an event which itself seems slightly out of the play's focus is significant. Variations of personality are sometimes obscured by Ada's reserve and withdrawal—as when, still affected by her father's sick accusations, she repulses Dave's attempts to comfort her—but in general such adjustment sinks so far into the background as to go unseen. [198]

Ada is if anything the more inflexibly idealistic of the two. This being so, the relevance of Libby Dobson's description of his two wives, who deteriorated mentally and spiritually into vegetative torpor or narrow petty-mindedness, is questionable. Although Ada says afterwards, "Do you realise he was talking about what I might become darling?" [189] nothing up to this point has suggested that her own strong and determined personality might disintegrate in this way. Indeed, excessive hardness seems a likelier pitfall: and in the event she is austere but sure-principled to the end of the play. So Libby's speech remains something of a red herring.

The time-scheme of the episodes still causes expository infelicities, such as Ronnie's "Nineteen forty-six! The war is really over isn't it, eh, Mother?" [159] But when further precise dating is necessary, the camouflage of Ada's letter-writing at the beginning of act two, and later of the wireless retailing Conservative successes in the General Election of

1959, are comparatively unobtrusive. More important is one's final impression of the play as somehow never achieving quite the same solidity as the other parts of the trilogy—although *Chicken Soup* spans a longer period, and in a larger number of scenes. This may be because Wesker's choice of scenes for *Jerusalem* tends to spotlight turning points in the action, and sometimes major crises—the arrival in Norfolk, Dave's dismissal, Sammy's departure, and Harry's second stroke—at the expense of more freely selected episodes which might have better expressed the everyday texture of the Simmonds' experience of rural life, the quality of which is, after all, the essence of their experiment. The play's naturalism, besides, is of a more old-fashioned, formalised kind, giving less weight to incidental activity on stage, or to casual dialogue, than its siblings. Thus, the house removal is active, but not routine, and even the vegetable-preparing by the aunts is out-of-the-ordinary. Because the quality of the Simmonds' *everyday* life is quite as significant to the theme of the play as that of the Kahns and Bryants, the value of documentary illustration, fully justified in the other plays, accordingly seems denied its proper place here.

3

Patterns of Failure

Chips with Everything and *Their Very Own and Golden City*

ALTHOUGH THE STRUGGLES of all Wesker's characters bear upon those of thousands of individuals, making his plays representative in the way that good plays always are, *Chips with Everything* is like *The Kitchen* in deserving to be called microcosmic, because for subject-matter it takes a social system in miniature. Here, the air-force hierarchy in a training camp for national servicemen as much represents "all the world" as *The Kitchen*—and this world is a more complicated one, more truly analogous to society in its stratified class system.

The action of the play, which opened at the Royal Court Theatre on 27th April 1962 and transferred to the Vaudeville in June for a successful West End run, centres on one of the latest batch of conscripts, Pip Thompson, who stubbornly chooses to stick to square-bashing with the working-class fellow-occupants of his hut—refusing the officer-training to which, as the son of a rich ex-Brigadier banker, his upbringing ought apparently to incline him. Rather, Pip seems set on inciting a mutiny against the unfair and irrational air-force system. He turns out, however, to be a rebel but not a revolutionary: he hates his father and the paternalistic officers, but basically (though perhaps unconsciously) he wants a reversal that will give *him* power, not destroy the power-structure itself. In the end, he joins the officer class he has failed to beat.

Thematically, the action involving Pip, because it deals primarily with the social relationship between ruler and ruled, needs the self-sufficiency, inclusive and inescapable, of its air-force context, to make its point fully. The rougher edges of larger society are here smoothed out, and there is not even the possibility of individual opting-out, such as Beatie's choice of escaping her family's petty-mindedness. The difference is that between Colonel Dewhurst's little brief authority in his specific sphere, and the Wing Commander's personification of authority absolute.

Obviously, class divisions, an inevitable corollary of ruler-ruled tensions, can be drawn up with beautiful simplicity within the air-force hierarchy, where rank is codified and the power of the resultant pecking-order is enforceable and enforced. But any coercion used is only partially enforceable: in practice it is imposed by the few on the many, and ultimately, therefore, through the consent or at least the apathy of the many. It is bluff, if you like. So the lesson—though it is never put into effect—is that of Pip's potted history of the French revolutionaries, who "suddenly looked at themselves and realised that there were more of them than they ever imagined". [30]

This is what gives Wesker's parable its vividness: for whereas the actual repressive workings of society are concealed by the theory of democracy, the sanction of law, unspoken tradition and ignorance, the army's power structure is naked and, for that matter, unashamed—a one-way transmission of decision and command, backed up by the obvious instruments of force and of immediate physical reprisals. But even here we are made to see that, in their numbers, the ruled are potentially more powerful than the rulers, dependent upon personal privileges—the same revelation as is poignantly glimpsed in the mutinies of *The Battleship Potemkin* and of Ernst Toller's *Draw the Fires*, where force of arms was, at last, employed by both sides, and the real odds glimpsed. Here, however, Corporal Hill can only say to the mutinous Pip: "Oh, thank your lucky stars this ain't the war, my lad; I'd take the greatest pleasure in shooting you." [62]

The opposing values in this ruler-ruled conflict are leadership on the one hand and unity on the other: and Pip's failure to transfer his allegiance from one to the other is his defeat. Apart from its basis in a sense of superiority unmistakably enough expressed, the leadership ideal of the officers depends on the existence of those to be led, and has as its sole purpose the trouble-free execution of necessary manœuvres. Even with good-nature on the part of the leaders, and admiration among the led, the relationship remains one of superior to inferior. "We slum for our own convenience", sums up the officers' attitude. [26]

Preservation of unity in, say, the hut in which the main conscript characters live, demands equality among all its occupants—so that common-feeling and corporate personality cannot easily be crystallised into any one spokesman or hero. This unity tends to be best suited to defensive endurance—the unity against outsiders that the Wing Commander despises. "They don't even fight seriously—a few loud words, and then they kiss each other's wounds." [35] It is less well adapted to aggressive action, which is partly why Pip's hut is not sympathetic to his subversiveness: "The boys will hate any heroic gesture you make." [63] But whether he is trying to make a private stand or a public example, Pip *is* acting as a leader, not as one unit of a simple whole.

Thus, the hierarchy of the camp is essential to the theme of the play, but its action and interest is not often closely associated with the officers, who make only isolated appearances. Rather, it catches up the nine national servicemen in Pip's own hut. Their particular unity is built up in their shared experiences, as much as in the relationships of the various personalities within the group: and its atmosphere is both created and verbally expressed in the quiet scene before the coke-stealing foray, as all nine and the corporal relax one evening. Andrew, the quiet-spoken Scots recruit, sums it up:

> I like us. All of us, here now. I like us all being together here. In a way you know I don't mind it, anything. Old Corp and his mouth-organ—all of us, just as we are, I like us.
> (*Pause. Mouth-organ. Warm hut.*) [47]

The political potentialities of this unity are hinted at in the Pilot Officers's half-misgiving, early in the play:

> I don't really frighten you, but you obey my orders, nevertheless. It's a funny thing. We have always ruled, but I suspect we've never frightened you. [25]

The threat surfaces during the Christmas party, and there is also a suggestion of it in Pip's "If . . . one of us is caught, then we all, all of us make an appearance. He can't cop the lot." [49] And there is, finally, a confrontation, a revolutionary situation of unity-as-defiance, which occurs as climax to the penultimate scene.

Theatrically, Pip's efforts to tap the source of this unity and his final inability to become part of it, overshadows the emergence of the unity itself. The first link in the tangled chain of events in which Pip catches himself up is his detailed recollection, in the second scene, of a visit to an East End café, which has evidently marked a kind of epiphany in his life. This lies uneasily at the root of his feelings towards the group: and beyond his revulsion, manifested in his hatred for the old man in the café who in spite of his conceded tidiness he remembers as ingrained with dirt, is a fascination with the amazing otherness of the milieu, a strangeness accepted in theory but overwhelming to the point of shock when really experienced.

His repeated exclamations of "Strange!" in this speech are directed against his own reflexes of surprise: and the bewildered incomprehension that causes this surprise pervades his description of the café. He cannot believe that anything about it has a real purpose or meaning, from the "weird patterns" the unclean cleaning-rag left on the table to the absurd, ritualistic eye-wiping of the old man. Pip's fascination is here established as essentially a reaction of unlike to unlike: it underlies the never-overcome alienation between him and the others in the body of the play. He winds up his recollection "You"—not "we"—"breed babies and you eat chips with everything." [16][25]

A weak spot in *Chips* coincides with its most overtly didactic episode, the Christmas party in the NAAFI. As all the scenes are distinct and self-contained, the set-piece nature of the party is not important—it is no more or less a set-piece than the balletic coke-stealing episode, which works well—but the scene does involve several improbabilities, and, in particular, inconsistencies of characterisation. As a counterbalance to the Wing Commander's contemptuous expectations of working-class culture—"a dirty recitation, or a pop song" [37]—Andrew's dialect rendering of a Burns poem is credible and impressive enough on its own terms to make the necessary point and possibly win over the other conscripts. However, the following folk song is far too little known for the assembly to join in spontaneously, and the symbolism of *The Cutty Wren* too obscure for even those who might conceivably pick up the chorus to understand the subversive point. Possibly this scene might be workable now if one of the popularised "protest songs" which caught on in the later sixties were substituted, and actually used and seen to be used *in a protest situation*. But, in addition, Pip's presentation of the episode as his own counter-offensive to a maliciously planned "experiment" on the Wing Commander's part is an unnecessary complication. The simple truth, that the men are being insultingly patronised, is all that needs asserting—and for that matter they are persuaded with an amazing ease that is itself almost patronising (on the author's part) to obey Pip.

Pip's next and most deliberately provocative gesture is his refusal to take part in bayonet drill—but this has little to do with his relationship with the rest of his hut, being more in the nature of an individual trial of strength with the officers. Truthfully he assures Andrew of this: "You don't really think I'm interested in the public spectacle, Andy, you can't?" [63] This gesture, not heroic but personal, anticipates his shout during the Pilot Officer's interrogation of him, "I WILL NOT BE AN OFFICER," [64] and is part of his duel with authority. His reactions and emotions during the Pilot Officer's final probing find fuller expression in their acted interpretation, of course, and in the text there is just the ambiguous "Oh, God." [65] Fortunately the context is broader than this one scene: for in the next scene Pip rescinds his refusal to carry out bayonet practice, and his friend Charles detects the considerable distress underlying the decision, in spite of Pip's silence:

Hell, look at your face, did they beat you? Did they make you use the bayonet? They did, didn't they? I can tell it from your face. You're crying—are you crying? [66]

For the P.O., analysing Pip, has eliminated all motives for his action, until the only one that seems to remain is the pursuit of power. That Pip is so stricken confirms the diagnosis. His gesture has failed, and thereafter his will to relate to the group fails too.

The scene with Charles, who wants their tentative friendship to grow, and be fruitful for him at least, proves at once that, as a motive, "the joy of imparting knowledge to your friends" [65] was accurately eliminated by the Pilot Officer. For Pip refuses. What Charles in effect is asking for is the Ronnie-Beatie style of education that succeeds because of the strength of the personal ties involved:

> I could grow with you, don't you understand that? We could do things together. You've got to be with someone, there's got to be someone you can trust, everyone finds someone and I found you. . . . [67]

This request and the burden of trust it carries, is almost a sacred obligation, and in *Their Very Own and Golden City*, Jake Latham responds to it with proper humility: but Pip shrugs it aside as insufficient. He interprets Charles's wish to learn as hopeless subservience, a wish simply to "swop masters". [68]

Unfortunately, the power motivation in Pip is perfunctorily sketched in. In the last analysis, what Pip does, as with most of Wesker's characters, shows what he is.[26] But such a welter of psychological explanation is offered for his behaviour—repulsion-fascination for the working class, oedipal rebellion, self-assertion, and finally, the desire for power—that this last (and probably truest) accusation by the P.O. carries relatively little weight. And, certainly, it is backed up by too little ballast in the way of retrospective dramatic evidence for the emotional reversal it causes in Pip to ring true—especially as the officers have been equally, falsely confident before of beating down his rebellion.

As a turning-point in the play, the scene with the Pilot Officer thus lacks the necessary dramatic conviction. But one earlier incident that does yield a convincing reinterpretation in this new motivational light is the raid on the coke-store. Pip puts himself in charge. After his "We'll work out a plan" and "Think we can't outwit them?" his choice of pronouns changes. "If you can't outwit them . . . they deserve to have you in here. . . ." And he concludes, "Trust me?" [47–8] Afterwards Charles and Dickey acknowledge that they "wouldn't have done it without Pip", [49] and couldn't "have pinched the coke without Pip's mind". And to this Corporal Hill adds, "You always need leaders." [50] Pip's vehement denial is then ironic in view of the leadership he has just assumed—and is to assume permanently in the end.

The scene which counterbalances the Pip-dominated coke raid is that during which Smiler, the fat, gormless-seeming recruit who has previously been the unhappy butt of his comrades' jokes and his superior officers' jibes, is tended lovingly by the rest of his hut after his abortive attempt at escape. This, together with the preceding episode, in which Smiler has paced out in desperate, weary words the circular escape route that has returned him to the camp, [68–70] puts into more serious perspective his hitherto rather comic sufferings: and after his return, the action picks out his place in the group, and its tendency to unite defensively to protect one of its members. As a development of the ruler-ruled relationship, Smiler's monologue expresses a range of attitudes like the Bryants' in *Roots*—resentment, wish to escape, incapacity to oppose or change. His hutmates, made conscious of the unthinking cruelty almost automatically inflicted on the weakest of their number respond first with care for Smiler, and the sense of this same helpless resentment, before a positively threatening move from the Pilot Officer provokes their defiance—thus unwittingly opposing Pip's feverishly contrived rebellion with their own genuine sense of cohesion and of the "affinity of one human being to another". [64]

This penultimate scene marks the true climax of the play. The silent, and now really dangerous confrontation between conscripts and officer, which Pip has been trying to engineer at various points throughout the play, has come about of itself, without even any reference to Pip. It is moreover Charles who initiates the defiance, and this both underlines Pip's new inertia and counters his earlier criticism of Charles's submissiveness. Although the principle of "he can't cop the lot" is not exactly accurate—"this whole hut is under arrest" [72]—obviously the involvement of nine conscripts en masse puts the incident into a much more serious light than that glowering over the single, insignificant Smiler. The explosive situation amounts to mutiny—but is gracefully defused by, of all people, Pip, who, interposing concessive praise at the cost of losing only a little face, tempers the provocative resistance the prospective mutineers have been meeting. The revolutionary situation is averted, and discontent or awareness damped down again, at least below flash-point level.

The completion here of Pip's reversal of roles—symbolically, he changes into officer's uniform while advising the P.O. how to deal with the men—follows his rejection of unobtrusive service to Charles, and his failure to take the lead or even participate in a movement not organised by himself. He finally cannot face being obliterated in a campaign of unindividualised mass protest, and he takes the side on which he can act with conspicuously clever initiative —in short, can show leadership. As Pip and the Pilot Officer "smile at each other, knowingly", [72] the officer's recognition of kinship proves itself. "We know—you and I—we know, Thompson." [65]

The brief closing scene adds nothing substantial to this, but makes a pertinent comment in the form of concealed irony. The flags, the sun, the band, and the Wing Commander's satisfaction are as impeccable as air-force tradition demands, and so—but only in the isolative sense—is the marching body of men. The juxtaposition with the previous scene, however, makes Corporal Hill's words begin to bite: "I want to see them all pointing one way, together—unity, unity." [74] For the unity requisite for efficient militarism is double-edged, and can be dangerous if turned against the minority of rulers. Hill goes on, "I want you to move as one man, as one ship, as one solid gliding ship." [74] And as the curtain falls, the audience's last glimpse is of a captive unity, the elephant under the tiny rider, immense but powerful, subject to the will of a weaker authority only as long as its unified will is subdued.

Since the action is at once more intensive in time and broader in its social canvas, few of the characters in this play are as gradually or exhaustively developed as the major three or four in *Chicken Soup* or *Jerusalem*. The dominant character, Pip, in order to keep his motives undisclosed—to himself, as to an audience—is necessarily enigmatic and opaque. He has nevertheless a marked personality that is not false or even superficial for being observed only from the outside. His characterisation according to what he *does*—including even the smallest outward responses to other characters—is at first difficult to understand because what he does is itself puzzling and often inconsistent. But this is because it is based on Pip's own unrealised inner contradiction. Charles thus becomes the character most readily knowable by an audience, resentful, impressionable, self-examining, and given to strong attachments like those he forms in different ways for Pip and for Smiler—the group personified.

There is less to know about the other conscripts, whose

personal depths of feeling have no bearing upon the main action of the play: but they must none the less exist as a group composed of sympathetic individuals. Without cataloguing their distinguishing traits, it is interesting to note that they not only have functional characteristics—Andrew the intelligent spokesman, Wilfe the life and soul of the party— but further non-essential yet rounding attributes. Thus, Andrew is analytic and poetic, while Wilfe is unemotionally perceptive ("you'd be just as helpless there . . . civvy street, the forces—it's the same, don't give me that"). [71]

The patterning of behaviour comes out most clearly in the characterisation of the officers: they are barely more than their official selves, archetypes of authority, whether in its insinuating or hectoring aspect, as set up for display in the lecture hall in the fourth scene. [21–4] This, Wesker has said, is intentional: he was "not going to make them rounded characters out of any sort of liberal impulse". And he admits that, in making the Wing Commander say, "Forget your theories about my unhappy childhood. Mine is a healthy and natural hatred," [35] his internal insistence on this lack of complication is deliberate clue-dropping on his part—"me, as author, cheating".[27] The officers, at once functions and characters, are thus conveniently consistent, to ensure the greater clarity-in-complexity of the other ranks, in dialogue as in action. And, because the real interest *is* centred on these other ranks, it is also formally entirely appropriate that the officers should appear to the audience as they do to the men—if not as identical, at least as identified by their positions, not their personalities.

Corporal Hill, betwixt and between, is rounded like the conscripts, not stereotyped like the officers. The variations in the Wing Commander's speeches between repression and tolerance are only apparent contradictions, which can, respectively, be resolved into sincere and purposely deceptive

modes of expression: but Hill's contradictions are real and
part of his character. He maintains his obvious control of the
hut by means of a certain ruthlessness, and he shares some of
the officers' attitudes. Thus, the Wing Commander's view
that "the men in your hut are slobs. Their standard is low
and I'm not satisfied. No man passes out of my camp unless
he's perfect—you know that," is duly reworked into his own
individualised echo:

> You're slobs, all of you. Your standard is low and I'm
> not satisfied. No man passes out of my hut unless he's
> perfect, I've told you that before. [59]

And Hill believes what he is saying. This being so, efficiency of training is high among his priorities—making
Smiler such an irritant to him that he initiates his persecu-
tion almost out of habit. On the other hand, he not only
feels a sense of identification with his hut, and some affection
for "his" boys, but his assessment of the relative seriousness of
bayonet drill and of death by shooting is more mature than
the frivolous playing at soldiers of the officers, who would
"sacrifice a million of them for the grace of a Javelin
Fighter". [32]

Corporal Hill's halfway position between officers and
men is a variation, from the other end of the class-scale,
upon Pip's emotionally ambiguous relations with both these
classes; but the relationship between Pip and Charles, which
is of a more equal kind, also holds up a mirror to social
tensions. Wesker suggests that Pip and Charles may derive
from two sides of himself:[28] and this helpfully points to their
complementary interaction. As Pip is fascinated by the
alien, dirty café world, so Charles is fascinated by Pip's
technicolour background of status and wealth. Slowly and
painfully they achieve communication in spite of—perhaps

because of—misunderstandings, and they agree that its basis is really the alive mind, not a cultivated respect for manual labour or for a ration of education. There may, too, be an undercurrent of erotic attraction in the establishment of this "between us" relationship, detectable particularly in Charles's initial antagonism and attraction, his later exultant admiration for Pip. Their attitudes towards each other expose pitfalls which threaten their supposed egalitarianism from both sides—Pip's tendency to patronise and instruct without teaching, Charles's touchy deference. In the event, Pip falls into the trap and Charles escapes; but because Pip is the more showy character, Charles's right-minded initiative—he is the first to act in Smiler's defence—doesn't have the balancing effect it might.

The unconcealed stylisation of the officers' characters, far more pronounced than that of, say, Colonel Dewhurst in *Jerusalem*, is not the only shift away from naturalism in *Chips*. There is an immense distance between the organised silence of the wordless action scenes in *Roots* and the silence of the coke-stealing expedition, which is put across with dramatic, spectacular, machine-like efficiency—and its own organic flourish. Wesker calls the convention he has followed in *Chips* "a kind of stylised naturalism":[29] and in many places the stylisation affects the idiom, so that impressive, poetic, or formal styles of speech fade in and out of the normally naturalistic dialogue without clear-cut division, thus developing the experiment of Beatie's early reminiscence of Ronnie in *Roots*. Smiler's running-speech is an exception, which combines stylisation of speech and action: the general effect of what he says is "natural" in that it is consistent in vocabulary and phrasing with his character, but in addition the speech runs the gamut of his confused rebellion, hate, bewilderment, self-pity and hope, so that his page-and-a-half of monologue telescopes the emotions and effort of his

entire roundabout escape from and return to the camp.
[68–70]

Elsewhere in *Chips*, the line is finely—and sometimes
problematically—drawn between conversational speech and
what an audience half registers as soliloquy, or thoughts the
speaker shares with it alone. The Pilot Officer shifts from
the public voice of "You aren't paid to think, Airman," to
what is not only the private but the unusually formal tone of
"We have always ruled, but I suspect we've never frightened
you." And, most confusingly, he winds up his musings to
Andrew with a threat, but again in formal, almost ritualistic-
ally abstract terms: "I shall not merely frighten you, there
are other ways—and you will need all your pity for yourself."
[25–6] Andrew is next seen repeating to the hut extracts
from all phases of the officer's speeches: implying that the
mandarin utterances have not only been heard but accepted
as unexceptional. Even more unusually formal is the Pilot
Officer's warning to Pip: "We listen but we do not hear, we
befriend but do not touch you, we applaud but we do not
act." [60] He repeats this, word for word, rhythm for
rhythm, a few scenes later: [64] and when Pip reports it to
Charles in the course of conversation, the latter queries its
meaning but not its form. [68]

Throughout the play the dialogue rises impressively above
the basic requirements of character differentiation. Apart
from such surface features as Dickey's quaintly polysyllabic
vocabulary, it is the underlying rhythm of the various speech
styles that essentially distinguishes character from character.
One of Corporal Hill's methods of domination is his
hypnotic outpouring of words. Two examples, the first from
the beginning of his speech in act one, scene three:

This is the square. We call it a square-bashing square. I
want to see you bash that square. Right, now the first

thing you've got to know, you've got to know how to come to attention, how to stand at ease and easy, how to make a right turn and how to step off.

Now to come to attention you move smartly, very smartly, to this position: heels together. STOP THAT! When I was born I was very fortunate, I was born with eyes in the back of my neck and don't be cheeky. [17]

And the second from the end of that same, long speech:

You nit, you nit, you creepy crawly nit. Don't you hear, don't you listen, can't you follow simple orders, CAN'T YOU? Shut up! Don't answer back! A young man like you, first thing in the morning, don't be rude, don't be rude. No one's being rude to you. [19]

The phrases usually flow one into another, the continuity reinforced by embellishments of rhythm marked by repetitions—"you move smartly, very smartly, to . . ."—and even the short sentences at the beginning of the first passage above are pulled together by these simple repetitions. In the second passage they give a smothering, overwhelming effect to the reprimand.

Contrast this with the Flight Sergeant's similarly simple hortatory remarks in the lecture hall:

As you were. I'm in charge of physical training on this camp. It's my duty to see that every minute muscle in your body is awake. Awake and ringing. Do you hear that? That's poetry! I want your body awake and ringing. . . . I hate thin men and detest fat ones. I want you like Greek Gods. You heard of the Greeks? You ignorant troupe of anaemics, you were brought up on tinned beans and television sets, weren't you? You haven't had any exercise since you played knock-a-down-ginger, have you? Greek Gods, you hear me? Till the sweat pours out of you like Niagara Falls. Did you hear that poetry? Sweat like Niagara Falls! I don't want your stupid questions! [23]

Here the opening sentences have their repetitious quality undercut as well as separated-out further by the self-conscious "that's poetry", and the subsequent sentences are distinct short statements or rhetorical questions, the idiom plainer and clipped much shorter than Corporal Hill's, so that each item aims at making its separate impact, in contrast with the Corporal's cumulative outpouring.

On the other hand, Pip's recollection of the East End café is a private, discursive narrative, which follows the form and flow of his thoughts. He is recounting a memory, as is Beatie in her speech about getting to know Ronnie, which occurs at a similarly early point in the play, though its information is less expository and more tangential. Like Beatie's, Pip's speech opens as factual narrative ("One day, when I was driving . . ."), then begins to interpose its irregularly repeated motif:

Strange—I don't know why I should have been surprised. Strange . . . WHY should I have been surprised? . . . But what I couldn't understand was why I should have been so surprised . . . [15–16]

The unhurried progress of the speech derives from the random, varied openings of the sentences and their comparative shortness (unlike the repetitious openings to the Flight Sergeant's short sentences, which emphasise their own brevity and the speaker's rigid control). The intimate, introspective tone is augmented by Pip's descriptions of idiosyncratic, inessential details, and these combine to shift the speech obliquely away from the logical or aggressive explanation expected in answer to Smiler's provocative: "You don't mind being a snob, do you?" [15] (If Pip's snobbery is a sense of otherness, it is an otherness that bewilders him.) This time the speech is not modulated back to a conventional conversational level but cut off short by the hiatus of Hill's entry.

The simple breaking-down of the plot-line into a series of different short scenes—instead of the accumulation, as in *Jerusalem*, of as much action as possible into a single scene in a single setting, to sustain the illusion of reality—is another benefit of the play's slight stylisation. This episodic organisation paradoxically increases one's impression of rapid flow, as each separate incident follows the last, at the same time as that flow is broken chronologically by the undisguised scene divisions. The divisions themselves are speeded up not only because their lack of naturalistic disguise cuts out the need for the raising and lowering of the curtain, but because Wesker has relaxed his habit of conscientious exposition. In fact the recognisable situation of the play and its usually sequential action make few demands on the author for added explanations: but a substantial amount is, all the same, left to the audience's observations.

Remarks designed to prepare the ground for a prospective new scene are, in fact, usually less obtrusive and less heavily informational than confirmatory comment afterwards. A typical example is the transition between act one, scenes six and seven:

GINGER: When's the Christmas Eve party?
DODGER: Tomorrow a week, isn't it?
HILL: Uh-huh.
   (*Continue sound of mouth-organ—change to—*

Scene 7

The NAAFI Christmas Eve Party. The rock'n'roll group play vigorously. The boys jiving, drinking and singing. Officers are present.

WING COM: Look at them. Conscripts! They bring nothing and they take nothing. Look at them. . . . [32]

Admittedly the Squadron Leader's second speech remarks that "it's a Christmas Eve party. We're guests here," [33] but this follows a half-page of exchanges during which the background of the party has already been established, so the speech isn't so bald as it seems out of context, and is in any case plausibly motivated. One example of nervous exposition that does survive occurs in Charles's later, superfluous comment that "The others have all gone to the NAAFI, it's New Year's Eve. . . ." [66] For this must be known to Pip already, and—since Corporal Hill wishes the boys Happy New Year later the same evening—the only excuse one can offer for the comment is that it might be self-conscious conversation-making. It's awkward to speak, anyway, and irrelevant as far as the audience is concerned.

But on the whole the scenes slip by one after the other with no faltering of pace due to technical hitches. A totally effective stylisation inspires transitions like that between the second and third scenes of the first act:

HILL: That's fast, that's fast, into the hut and move that fast. Into the hut, in, in, into the hut. (*Looks at watch. Pause.*) Out! I'll give you . . .

Scene 3

Parade Ground: morning.

HILL: Out! I'll give you sixty seconds. . . . [16]

Equally happy is the theatrical flourish which has Pip and Charles diverging into parallel musings aloud. These first detect the analogy between their respective revulsions against the labouring and the intellectual pose. "It's no good wanting to go to university . . . Like me and work—manual labour." [44] Each man then pursues his own pet hate, more in irritation than communication, but "they smile" in understanding at the end. [45] This lacks the denseness and unconscious irony of the dovetailing of the duologue in *The Friends*, but the recognised analogy gives the separate preoccupations a felicitous tonal harmony.

The desultory, semi-poetic soliloquies, the often self-parodying passages of army routine, the backchat and misunderstandings of the conscripts in the hut, combine to make this play Wesker's most pinteresque in verbal texture, and although the sharply intellectual thematic development of *Chips* is in marked contrast with the way in which Pinter deploys his material, perhaps the oblique, ambivalent, half-conscious relationships that make their occasional shadowy emergence—between Charles and Pip, Pip and the Pilot Officer, Smiler and Wilfe—are closer to dealing, as does Pinter, with the elusive, irrational, unconquerable pressures of life. Increasingly, too, the unreliability of a character's behaviour—his tendency to be betrayed by his own unsuspected, uncontrollable weaknesses—comes to influence the public as well as the domestic action of the plays: and Wesker was to probe this interaction as it influenced one man's whole life and work in his next play, *Their Very Own and Golden City*.

However pronounced the parallels between *Chicken Soup* and *Ghosts*, Nora Helmer can't easily be superimposed upon Beatie Bryant, nor *Rosmersholm* on *Jerusalem*. But in *Their Very Own and Golden City*, first performed in England at the Royal Court Theatre on 19th May 1966, Wesker's architect-hero Andrew Cobham does have a little in common with Ibsen's Masterbuilder Solness—his spiritual hovering between inspirational and down-to-earth architecture, his estranged wife, his susceptibility to guidance from another strong-minded woman. Characteristically, however, Ibsen's Masterbuilder dies dramatically at the final curtain, whereas Wesker's patchwork idealist declines into rancorous old age, a recurrent vision of his hopeful past (built into the play's structure) preventing it from toppling over into unalloyed pessimism.

Andrew Cobham qualifies as an architect while working as a draughtsman apprentice. His aspirations range from giving his wife Jessie "a house that soars" [14] to reconstructing society by rebuilding its cities. So he dedicates himself—at the expense, it turns out, of a far-from-soaring home life—to providing real homes for human beings, in a proposed, visionary scheme of six "golden cities". These are to be exhilaratingly beautiful, to belong to their inhabitants, houses, factories and all—in short, to be in every way designed to further the good life. But only one city is built, and it is in various ways a compromise. Cobham himself is transformed, virtually broken, by the long struggle.

The unifying concern of *Golden City* had been dramatised before by Wesker in *The Kitchen, Chicken Soup* and *Jerusalem*, even in *Chips*, but never so starkly as here: and the impotence which attends the preservation of a pure ideal is weighed against the limited effectiveness of a corrupting compromise, in a dilemma larger in scale than Sarah Kahn's or the Simmonds'. Indeed, in *Golden City* Wesker asserts this theme so insistently that the *principles* of the ideal-compromise conflict—as distinct from its resolution—are unmistakable. At the same time, because the disadvantages on both sides are very clear—though not over-schematic—an audience is discouraged even from temporary indulgence in stock responses:

whilst, in parallel, the long development of the Golden
Cities project mirrors the development of Andrew Cobham's
own character. But perhaps it is only half true to say that
Andy is warped by the stresses of the Golden City: equally,
the Golden City is itself progressively changed by its creator's
fluctuating strength and purity of intention. And of course
this enervating reciprocity is aptly illustrative of the thematic
man-environment interaction, an interaction that even the
characters as city-builders do (in theory) recognise.

All we actually witness on the stage, however, is the unfolding of Andy's life: the eponymous image of the play
remains (as in *The Cherry Orchard*) elusively, allusively, just
off-stage, or glimpsed obscurely from the fringes of a building
site. The progress of the play is episodic, proceeding like
Chips by means of short scenes, which here illustrate stage
after stage in Andy's life over the longest time-span of all
the plays—the sixty-odd years from 1926 to a still-recognisable
1990. The play opens as Andy—a very young man—together
with his future wife Jessie, and two friends from schooldays,
Stoney and Paul, picnic and sketch in Durham Cathedral:
and it closes as Andy reaches old age, achieves public
honours, and reaps only personal bitterness.

This basic pattern is elaborated first by the interspersing
of the chronological sequence of scenes in act one with
occasional flashbacks to the opening situation in the cathedral; and in this way the ageing friends are from time to
time juxtaposed with their youthful selves. Then, in act two,
which covers the years from 1947 to 1990, there is just one
self-contained flashback, in scene four, whilst in scene six
the years from 1948 to 1990 follow in a single, more fluid
movement. Here, the prophetic "flash-forward" technique
shifts the action stage by short stage into the future, but it is
specified that no formal scene division should be sensed
between sequences: and the significance of the increase in

fluidity achieved by overlapping hitherto distinct breaks is explained in Wesker's own note to act two, scene six, in which he requires "a sense of purpose, bustle, activity and—most important—growth and decay". [64]

In effect, the first act interposes a definite, felt break between one scene and the next, even if these are linked by a similar conversation or take up the same situation: note, for example, the *Chips*-like transition between scenes two and three, the earlier scene ending as "Andy stands on his head," and the scene changing to a "riverside, some hours later. Andy still on his head." [19] But changes of setting in the continuous scene are quicker and more dream-like:

> The party breaks up. Only Andy is left. The thuds and scrapings heard from a building site now echo. Stoney and Paul join Andy to address the 300th Monday Meeting. [72]

The former transition is a cut, the latter a mix, and Wesker's note tries to define the effect sought after, at once deliberate and vertiginous:

> Towards the end of each situation (set), preparation will be going on for the next situation (set), so that characters will turn immediately from one phase of the development to another. It must appear as one continuous movement, slowly and inexorably unfolding—rather like watching the painting of Dorian Gray slowly change from a young man into an old and evil man—as in the film. [64–5]

This, then, is the play's formal framework. In *Chips*, the free-wheeling, uncluttered mobility of the episodic form had been what Wesker utilised: here, he exploits its possibilities more fully. Scenic juxtaposition in *Chips* is a technique of moving smoothly from one stage of the action to the next:

here, it is itself a means of presenting parallels and contrasts.

Sometimes a word or phrase, echoed from one scene to the next, simply points to continuity of topic—as in the "teach me" transition between scenes four and five of the first act. [24] But often such a continuity of topic involves a shift of perspective as well as of scene. Thus, in the play's opening two scenes it is an easy step from the cathedral to the office where Andy's first employer Casper is trying to divert his mind from his imminently expected examination results with a display of designs—and in the cathedral Andy had jokingly predicted just such a scene. This is in itself only a superficial continuity: more organically, Andy concludes the cathedral scene by exclaiming, "Dear God, look how that ceiling soars," whilst his first response to Casper's proffered design in the next scene is that "it doesn't soar though, does it?" [17] Soaring is inspirational in the play: the soaring cathedral enshrines Andy's first aspirations, whereas the humdrum office of kind, gentle Mr Casper does not. Vision and dreary "dull caution" [52] are already pitted against each other, and so weighted as to underlie and explain Andy's first choice, his decision not to stay with Casper.

Thus, part of the play's central conflict is reflected in scenes that rebound from affirmation of inspired creativity to attacks on the rest of the world's inertia. But such an externalised conflict is less important than the complexities within Andy himself. The interaction between the development of the Golden City and its creator's integrity is, as we have said, traced only in the life of that creator: but this duality of action and character is separated out again *within* Andy, respectively in his public and private lives—his public career including his professional work specifically as an architect, and his involvement in politics generally, as well as his professional-cum-political campaigning for the Golden Cities.

So, after his decision not to dilute his purposeful enthusiasm with dull, safe work for Casper, the Andy of 1947 is to be found struggling with the mean-spirited council that now employs him—as, apparently, he has been struggling throughout the thirties. Then, later still, he agrees to design buildings he despises, sacrificing professional integrity to the City's financial needs. On the political front, Andy appears at a trade union branch meeting, speaks in an important debate in his local Labour Party, and—immediately before the continuous scene, making this a felt turning-point of the action—addresses the Trades Union Congress. (The parallels between his career and Wesker's own campaign for Centre Forty-Two are clear, but critically irrelevant, and often actually misleading: they are best ignored.[30]

Underpinning the decisions and actions of the public scenes are the episodes of domestic life, including to some extent the scenes which show Andy with his friends—and, particularly, with his wife, Jessie, and with Kate, the "class-less" daughter of a local landowner, who loves him. The relationship between the public and private scenes is again both direct and indirect. On two occasions Kate, out walking with Andy, puts into or strengthens in his mind certain plans or convictions—to become a councillor, or to inaugurate the Golden Cities on his own. And so the episode during which Andy explores the frustrations of his life, prompting Kate to suggest that he stand for the council, is followed by three scenes of conflict in which Andy, finding it necessary to oppose his friend and mentor Jake Latham on a matter of policy and morality, begins to realise the constraints upon effectual action. There is a straightforward continuity of topic: and although the implications of the theory-practice maladjustment, intimately connected with the main theme of the play, are less overtly suggested, they are clear in Stoney's remark, "Politics is your game now—here's your first big dilemma: eve of poll and your closest friend has decided to take a stand on his own." [40]

Less explicit, though, is the still earlier scene in which Andy's picnic with the young Jessie—"simple like a cottage loaf and pure-smelling like a rose" [21]—is disturbed by forebodings of the coming war. This is Andy's last speech:

It's just—I'm thinking that near by it sounds like such a dreadful war that all I want to do is eat the cottage loaf and smell the rose. [21]

But the next scene shows him some months later, a new member at his trade union branch meeting, soliciting instruction from Jake Latham: and here the juxtaposition is plainly significant of both Andy's character and of the dialectic development of the play.

The influences work both ways, reflecting the reciprocity between the City and its creator. So, in the second act Kate demands ruthless pragmatism from Andy, to the exclusion of all conflicting private interests—and in the following scene he makes the professional decision to supplement the Golden City's funds by supplying hack designs on demand, the domestic consequences of which are foreseen by Jessie:

Andrew Cobham, as the years go on it gets harder and harder to live with you. I'll not have you grunting and storming through this house because you're building a building you don't want to build. You, with a screaming and snapping head above what you are, is more than I can bear. . . . [68]

And this effect on Andy's temper is only too accurately predicted—as the Conservative politician Maitland (a more reasonable reactionary than most of his kind in Wesker's work) notices, even when he is offering financial help:

I can't say I shall look forward to speaking to him. He'll snap. He snaps all the time. You all snap—been at it too long, Kate. All of you, a whole lifetime. He'll snap. [80]

This speech precedes the transition to a "situation" in Andy's home, during which his "snapping" at Jessie progressively reveals itself as a device for escaping from her more pertinent questions, and, indeed, as a means of disengaging himself from her altogether.

Golden City, then, is about the incarnation of ideals in impure form. But integrated with or overlapping this theme is the theme of *The Kitchen* and *Roots*—the fragmentation, the lack of unity, which diminishes or destroys the lives of the majority. I mention the point here because, obviously, the practice of distinguishing vision from necessary compromise becomes a cancerous destroyer of Andy's integrity: and the more areas of life he can rule off and dismiss as not worth sensitive and honest attention, the more unreliable do his resources of sensitivity and honesty become for those purposes he does deem worthy his "uncorrupted" notice.

In act one, Andy believed that there was

something about people getting together and doing things . . . I don't see the point of insisting you're an individual—you're born one anyway . . . But a group together, depending on each other, knowing what they want, knowing how to get it— . . . But a group together . . . Now that's something. [32–3]

Later, after basic disagreements of principle, Paul and Stoney become estranged from Andy. Jessie asks about them, and in the asking reasserts her own claims to consideration:

Why do they stay away from here? . . . There was a time when your work kept you all together. . . . Friendship is a

beautiful thing, you once said; people who share your—
I'm sorry, I disturb you, don't I?

But Andy's attitude has noticeably shifted:

Share, share! Everybody wants to share, everyone wants
a bit of your peace or your love. Share? You share my
bed. [81]

And the disjunction is what Kate had demanded earlier, in
the interests of single-minded devotion to essentials:

Your decisions, any decisions you make, affect this project.
I charge you again—your family is your family and your
work is your work, and you have not the right, no right at
all, to neglect a project involving so many for the sake of
your own good life . . . I warn you, those of us who build
the Golden City can never live in it, never. [67]

Ironically, however, because of the actual interaction of all
parts of Andy's life, this cultivated callousness on the domestic
front infects his spiritual guardianship of the Golden City.
At last, dissociation culminates in the octogenarian Andy's
grimly fine soliloquy, in which his misanthropic howls are
muted by his alienation from man, the gods, the whole of
the universe, and in which any noble indignation has long
since been eroded by disillusion:

I shall stay just still like, petrified, because I won't be able
to find a single reason why I should make one word follow
another, one thought follow another. [88]

The process of entropy is complete.
The complex choices that have led Andy to this point plot

the course of the play's action, and determine its thematic emphasis. This is shaped early in the play by Jake Latham, retiring as a trade union branch chairman, who asks simply whether it is "better to risk defeat in defence of a principle or hang on with compromises?" [26] True, his phrasing itself suggests that "risk", "defence" and "principle" connote more admirably than "hang on" and "compromises". Equally true, Andy proceeds to *make* compromises, and ends up an embittered, dissatisfied old man. If this were all, the answer to Jake's question would be simple, and its elaborate illustration in the play either naïve or unnecessary. But to some extent, even if six Golden Cities had been built, they would all have been compromises compared with the real alternative to patchwork solutions—"that complete revolution we all used to talk about". [59] As the chairman of Andy's planning committee puts it, "you're asking us to change our whole society". [51] And for that matter, asking for "the international control of the seas and an economic pact throughout the world which would control the source of our raw materials". These Andy, by implication, is declaring to be impossible, [46] so that when he turns to the idea of total cities after despairing of patchwork, the chairman of the committee can legitimately point out: "*You* know why the cities won't work—them's also patchwork." [52]

Of course, we too have to understand that the really pure ideal—an instantaneous new society—is unattainable, and, *practically*, offers nothing better, as Andy has realised: "There's no situation that's revolutionary, is there? Face it, all of you. There-is-no-revolutionary-situation." [59] So that avoiding compromise here would lead, classically, to total immobility. Is the whole project a tragic mistake, then, a corrupt and therefore doomed compromise from start to finish? And is the "message" of *Golden City* that one might as well stay out of harm's way by doing nothing?

Wesker purposely allows Andy to recognise the dilemma and to choose consciously to act against reason in hope of a miracle:

> In the way you build a city you build the habits of a way of life in that city—that's a fact. Six Golden Cities could lay the foundations of a new way of life for all society—that's a lie, but that's the lie we're going to perpetuate, with our fingers crossed. [59]

The lie becomes a test of faith:

> If I decide to build those cities, then I'll forget they could ever have been regarded as patchwork, I'll ignore history. [59]

But this is something an audience must not forget, lest it too be tricked, like Andy, into regarding the cities as real utopias, worth any sacrifice.

For all the discouragement, ultimately despair, that the project breeds, such a defiance of history, a devotion to a goal as perfect as possible, has a certain intrinsic nobility. Paradoxically, in this play each of the alternatives, the ideal and the compromise, must be judged by results. And if the illustrations and images the characters use for the ideal or vision are considered carefully, each time some result—*not* immobility—is forthcoming. The only unwavering examples of idealism that are singled out for praise or blame—whether for what the first farm labourers' union did do, or for what Ramsay MacDonald's government did not do—are those which eventually had some tangible result, as an inspiration, positive or negative, for future, effective action. Such concealed pragmatism is expounded in Jake Latham's reply to his own question:

People always need to know that someone was around who acted. Defeat doesn't matter; in the long run all defeat is temporary. It doesn't matter about present generations but future ones always want to look back and know that someone was around acting on principle. [26]

And this, the historical, albeit indirect consequence of enacted idealism, makes the lengthy time-span, and the *structural* retrospection which is integral to *Golden City*, all the more important.

As well as the argument of example, even the example of martyrdom, the interaction between deeds and doers examined above is another prudent reason for uncompromising integrity. To get anywhere near achieving his vision with the means to hand, Andy needs a delicacy of balance of which he is not really capable: and this emerges clearly from the clash with Jake Latham at the Labour Party meeting. Kate has remarked of Andy's cautious habit of planning ten moves ahead that he is still not proof against risk, "because if the first move is wrong, he's gambled away the next nine". [35] And in the debate at the meeting I think one can find the crucial point at which Andy loses his complete freedom—his behaviour here slightly predisposing him to make the wrong choice next time.

His friend Jake threatens just before the council elections to split the local party by supporting a resolution in favour of halting re-armament against the Nazi threat: but Andy's speech outmanœuvres Jake, and reunites the party. Now in terms of this particular incident, Jake's idealistic disregard for the possibility of defeat is plainly delusive, as an audience's hindsight as well as Andy's arguments show. So is Andy right? The qualified answer is that we see a man who lacks defences against the ill effects of compromise: his reactions are coarse, and, in dirtying his hands, he fails to see the need to keep them at least no dirtier than necessary. He has achieved his own debating victory ostensibly by relying on facts, but rhetorically by sacrificing Jake as a man to ridicule. Jake perceives this, and warns him to "be careful of your cities . . ." [47] Prophetically, as it proves.

Coarse responses here are symptomatic of Andy's increasingly one-sided devotion to the tangible aspects of his city-building, and dissociation of ideas again fragments his vision. Jake had gently mocked the young Andy for failing to consider certain vital elements of his city's well-being: "How interesting. You want to build cities but you don't want to know about economics." [25] And Andy finishes up by fastening on to a limited conception of the city as the sum of its buildings, losing again both the spirit and economic heart which was its original purpose. Kate, as often happens, is the first to state baldly a position which, after vacillation, Andy comes to accept. She is minimising the importance of a compromise which will prevent the city dwellers from controlling their own means of production:

Compromise? What compromise? That the workers won't own the factory they work in? As if it makes much difference whether they own the machine or not, they'll still hate it. Do you really imagine I ever believed such things would make a city golden? It'll be beautiful—enough! There'll be no city like it in the world. They'll come from the four corners—it'll be beautiful and that will be enough. [79]

Not Jerusalem the Golden, merely the Golden Calf. A new way of life for a whole community becomes a prestigious exercise in town planning.

The development of Andy's character in relation to a dominant thematic image—here, the Golden City—is as deliberate and consistent as that of Harry Kahn or of Beatie Bryant. Determined, electrically energetic youth evolves into dogged, smouldering age: and the dramatic conviction of this development is rigorously tested by the flashback sequences, their frequent glimpses of the original Andy acting as a continuous correlative.[31] In some ways, *Golden City* is *The Four Seasons* turned inside out: the former is the more complete in its panorama of the public and private influences upon its main characters' lives, but it drastically selects and subordinates these private elements, whereas *The Four Seasons* is set physically within its own isolated, intimate, introspective world. Yet Andy here, and Adam in *The Four Seasons*, are really similar characters, only the difference in thematic perspective (the choice of situations in which they are shown in action) projecting Andy's active determination as opposed to Adam's vulnerability.

Throughout the play Kate has meant well, but her attitude has driven (and represented) the wedge between the spirit of the project and the form it takes. Divisiveness is an active force in her character, more active even than her harshness or ruthlessness: she is tough-minded enough to despise worship of the common man—to her, as to Pip in *Chips* and several of the characters in *The Friends*, the cult is a sentimental denial of standards—yet this at first salutary honesty is adapted by Andy into an excuse for his own ever-increasing alienation from other people.

A lot of Kate's attacks are given their force mainly by word-play. Thus, her criticism of the young Andy's land-lady and her admittedly mediocre taste is superficially clever, but utterly ignores Andy's objection to it: "Personal things count for me. That's a truth also—attachments count." [30] And two scenes later she is juggling labels with political facility: "Look at your emancipated working class, leaping to adopt the values of simpering shopkeepers. . . . I don't attack a class, only certain kinds of human beings." [35] Class, kind, type—ultimately these are only different ways of slicing the same cake. Her appeal for professionalism—or specialisation—is equally divisive in its instant appeal.

Why should the man who buys his city know how to build it? Why shouldn't we turn to you for our homes, to the poet for his words, to the Church for its guidance? Participation? It's a sop, dear, to ease your conscience. [58]

The argument turns on the phrase "how to build": because the architect knows "how to build", Kate is ready to concede his right to decide *what* is to be built, and what is good for the inhabitants of a building.

Yet a recollection of the actual differences between the priorities of most architects and most house dwellers, as between the deepest preoccupations of poets and readers or the sense of spiritual need of churchmen and laymen, reminds one how partial a qualification knowing "how" to build actually is. And, significantly, professionalism is here used to justify Andy's arbitrary control of the way of life he is to engineer, though earlier he has professionally categorised politicians as "men we hire to mend roads and tend to the sewers", [39] precisely in order to rule out their claims to interfere with his own "consumer's" social vision.

Kate's decisive manner, her snap judgements, give an impression of a strong character: but her strength, unlike, say, Ada's in *Jerusalem*, is manifested in her need for ceaseless activity—she makes clothes, although she "can't bear manual labour", because "it relieves my boredom and softens my temper". [36] Typically, as here, her dialogue is tense with organisation: there are no casual remarks, only communications streamlined to convey incisively a maximum of information. Her speeches, whether argumentative or conversational, are always purposeful and this, which in naturalistic plays can often be a sign of stylistic awkwardness, is what helps give her character its necessary, uncomfortable sense of suppressed energy.

There is, however, more to the character of Kate than this outline of the managing "other woman". For all her ambition and capability, most of her activity in the play is vicarious and peripheral: there is no reason why a determined, rich young woman during the thirties should not have realised her pioneering aims and beliefs through her own career, instead of manipulating the lives of clever male acquaintances. The explanation is that, just as much as Jessie, but more subtly, she is a woman whose life has been spoiled and stunted by Andy and the Golden City: to Jessie at the end of the play Kate seems a victimiser, but she, like Andy, is also a victim. The eagerness and arrogance of her youth must be recognised as not necessarily repellent but even endearing absurdities, and this makes the attraction she has for Andy and the deterioration of her own life comprehensible and consistent. Similarly, her attacks on Jessie's housewifely competence and on Andy's interest in his own home life are motivated as much by simple jealousy as by ruthlessness.

Jessie herself provides an embodiment of those otherwise off-stage, down-trodden wives like Libby Dobson's in *Jerusalem*, Adam's in *The Four Seasons*, and Macey's in *The Friends*: so that, in her case, Andy's abrupt dismissals are balanced by her own points of view. Jessie's relegation to the ranks of the dull and unimportant is painful because, not being complacent, incompetent or obtuse, she feels the relegation bitterly herself. She has known Andy and his friends from their youth, and cannot be as deferential as Beatie Bryant towards the more alien Ronnie. Here, early in the play, she protests at Andy's one-sided praise of her:

Simple! Simple! Cottage loaves and apple dumplings! You don't think me foolish by any chance? I mean I'd not be happy knowing we were married just 'cos we've been together these years. You wouldn't marry anyone you thought a fool—you wouldn't, would you, would you, Andy? [21]

Andy evidently would: but whether from habit or some less conscious, psychological perversity is less clear than the drawn-out consequences—the years of mutual wearing-down and wearing-out.

The emotional opposition represented by Kate and Jessie does more than complete an eternal triangle, or illustrate sides of Andy's character: the relative dominance of the two women during the course of the play is a measure of what becomes important in the plans for the Golden City. Jessie is given a forceful speech of protest towards the end of the play—the more forceful because of a faulty articulacy that is itself part of its meaning:

I'm not a fool; I've been made to feel it often enough, but I'm not a fool, even though I think you're right all the time, and—oh, if only I had the powers to argue and work it out—there's a wrong somewhere.

You said find your rightful place, I've found it. You said accept your limitations, I've accepted them—people should be happy with their limitations, you said. Happy! Me, happy! My only reward is to be treated like a hired housekeeper instead of your wife. . . .

Don't you know what I'm saying? Don't you hear what I'm telling? I don't mind being inferior but I can't bear being made to feel inferior. I know I'm only a housekeeper but I can't bear being treated like one.

Wasn't it you wanted to treat everyone like an aristocrat? Well, what about me? I don't claim it as a wife, forget I'm your wife, but a human being. I claim it, as a human being. . . . Claim? I'm too old to stake claims, aren't I? Like wanting to be beautiful, or enthusiastic or in love with yourself. [82]

This speech clarifies not only Jessie's deep hurt, but the loss of human sympathy and fellow-feeling that is at the basis of the failure of the Cities. Their original purpose had been to serve the people who would live in them: *that* is what they were to have been comfortable, beautiful, revolutionary *for*. Andy's Golden Jerusalem is as much a metaphor for the life within as Dave Simmonds', and his tragedy lies in forgetting this.

The minor characters are as competently drawn as the conscripts in *Chips*, their traits selected or spotlighted for a certain purpose in the play but another dimension suggested through hints of complexities beyond the focus of the action—such as Stoney's ambivalence towards the constant flow of love his clerical vocation requires. Jake Latham, in particular, the most important minor character, illustrates Wesker's power to animate an apparent stereotype: shrewd, wise, humorous, he is the self-taught, experienced, committed working-man, almost a class myth-figure. Yet the epithets take on life in his dialogue. He is quick to shoot back at the young Andy's search for knowledge: "Are you patronising me, young lad, are you?" [24] Yet he modulates his tone at once into sober humility when Andy asks if it is every day someone comes to him asking to be taught. "No. Never, actually. No one's ever given me such a responsibility. Laugh, do I? Daft old man, me." [25] And, in full spate as he elaborates the crucial compromise-versus-principle problem (with undeniable "shrewdness" and "wisdom"), he scoops up Andy's interjected "Do you want me to answer?"

with an unchecked "Of course not, just listen." [26] Jake is self-aware, unperturbed, and *alive*.

Produced after *The Four Seasons* but written concurrently with it, and conceived and begun much earlier, *Golden City* has absorbed into its naturalistic north-eastern rhythms (more strictly accurate than the stagier vowel-distortions of *The Friends*) the same capacity for striking out fresh phrases with haunting sounds that was to distinguish Adam and Beatrice's language in the later play. On the level of epigram, Jake rejects Andy's "jargon". "Don't confuse breathing new life with the perpetuation of stale breath," he says, though Andy, with equal pertinency, replies, "You prefer homely maxims to jargon, is it?" [23] And the trade union leader Bill Matheson comments on the "pretty words" the city-builders use: they have just been describing how "the walls rise and the flowers blossom", bringing "all the patterns men make for the pleasure of their living". [72–3] Apart from evocative description, the compelling music in, for instance, the alliteration of that last phrase infuses with poetry speeches which are already rhetorically effective.

Consider, too, the following passage:

We should have answers and not be doubled up by despair. Old age laments, leave lamentations till the grave—*we* know? *We* know what holds men in a movement through all time—their visions. Visions, visions, visions! [63]

Here, all the *l*'s of "Old age laments . . ." slide away into the grave, and the see-saw intonation of interrogative and positive in "*We* know? *We* know . . ." lifts the cadence again, ready for the cumulative "visions!" There is incantatory force in the continuing alliterative patterns:

But men have minds which some good God has given so we can tackle problems bigger than our daily needs,

so we can dream. Who dares tell us we've no right to
dream? The dull and dreary men? Then tell the dull and
dreary men to crawl away. [63]

And this leads into the peroration, with its repeated refrain
of "we have a city". The idiom exemplifies more than a
technique of public speaking: though vehement and polemical, it is the urgent expression of a private vision become
public, the public poetry of exhortation.

The visual images which predicate the verbalised themes
of *Golden City* are more successful than the slightly anonymous,
too archetypal house setting Wesker chose for *The Four
Seasons*, since this contained either too much or too little to
be effective. The building symbols are obviously appropriate
for an architect protagonist, yet are both subtler and more
direct than, say, Masterbuilder Solness's phallic towers.
The Cathedral itself is a place for, and a representation of,
worship and inspiration, just as the Golden City is to house
and represent a social ideal. Unfortunately, in the original
London production the predominantly black, white and
grey designs were less in harmony with the concept of the
Golden City than with the chaste, austere projection of
Durham Cathedral, which thus appeared much more
impressive and numinous. The Golden City is never seen,
and perhaps its unfinished, dwindling reality, all the while its
builders are extolling and projecting it, puts the verbal
descriptions in hazard of never quite prevailing over the
drab offices and lecture halls in which they are spoken. The
City's single realisation on stage is as a building site, which
is exciting without being exactly evocative of beauty.

The play ends on a typically ambiguous note, juxtaposing
the warning of the distant future with the confidence of the
distant past. The warning is against seduction by the outward form of any vision. Old Sir Andrew Cobham is left in

his chair, and the closing scene returns to the Cathedral, where, symbolically, the four young characters have been accidentally locked in. "I can't believe there's not one door open in this place," says Andy. And in this case there *is* a door: Paul has found a way out, and the friends escape confidently. "We knew the door was open." [90–1] The Cathedral, which throughout the play has been an image for the youthful vision, yet which is also a forerunner of the secular image, the Golden City, has threatened to turn at last into a prison: and on the defiant note of hope at the end, we realise also that the characters are seeking not to construct or enter into, but to escape from, an empty building that can only contain, or imitate, the living truth.

4

Private Pain

The Four Seasons and *The Friends*

THE TIME SPANS of Wesker's plays extend from *The Kitchen*'s one working day to the episodic, sixty years' history traced by *Their Very Own and Golden City*. *Roots*, as in so many ways, is the exception, in that it develops over an unstructured but brief period, and in this it approaches nearest to the haphazard "one morning . . . one week later . . . the following evening" chronology of the run-of-the-mill Shaftesbury Avenue play. *The Kitchen* and *The Friends* are shorter, and are like *Roots* in developing their situations and working towards their crises briskly. But the neoclassic, twenty-four hour limits within which these, Wesker's first and latest plays, are bounded obviously have an intentional importance in implying recurrence, typicality, concentration: whereas time *as such* in *Roots* is not thus integral to the theme. Time passing, over years or hours, usually has this crucial significance to Wesker's work because it indicates or implies change, choice, altering circumstances, with which are counterpointed routine and repetition—the elements that are most influential in shaping his characters' lives.

In spite of its year-long development, *The Four Seasons*—which was first staged in London at the Saville Theatre on 21st September 1965—is closest to *The Kitchen* in the way that its time-scheme functions. Its poetic, deliberately formalised patterning is in sharp contrast to the detailed,

proliferative naturalism of the Trilogy: its stripped sequences
are weighted with significance, and method and meaning
are even more closely associated than in *Chips*. Episodes that
in the other plays are spaced over years more often than
weeks are here fitted formally and evenly into the four seasons
of one year—a period which, like one working day, or, to a
lesser extent, like the eight-week training period of *Chips*,
is anonymous but typical. What is even more pertinent,
however, is that a year is also cyclical—revolving, unchang-
ing. *The Four Seasons* is as much a cautious illustration of
failure as the other plays (with the exception of *Roots*),
but its cyclical framework suggests an eternal *recurrence* of
failure, so that the action yields not even an open verdict,
but an iron judgement on past and future.

Here, then, Wesker really has written a "pessimistic"
play. The seasons recur, and bring round again an unvarying,
obviously imperfect condition of things—a condition that is
part of people, who are incapable of change, or of being
changed. The only two characters, Adam and Beatrice, act
out a love affair within this single year's cycle, the phases
of the affair emerging, growing, blossoming and dying
within the four natural scene divisions of Winter, Spring,
Summer and Autumn. Seasonally, this is a repetition of
earlier love affairs, similarly patterned, equally embittered.
Adam notices that his best efforts are powerless to alter the
sequence: "And I try to believe it can't be true, not all the
time, but it is." [35] Instead of hints of possibly better choices,
of reversals that could have changed everything, such as
occur even in *The Kitchen*, the only changes are intensifica-
tions of the worst suffering that burn the pattern deeper.
"Moments like these remind me that time passes and time
passing reminds me of sadness and waste and neglect and
suffering." [57]

Thus, the failure of Adam and Beatrice differs from the

failures of Ronnie, Dave or Pip, because it is presented as not
circumstantial but inevitable—it is universalised by the
seasonal cycle, the elimination of differentiating social
conditions, the absence of any qualifying element of optimism in the theme. Wesker has stressed that the play was meant
to dramatise private pain, and that he did not intend his
two characters to connote, archetypally, Man and Woman:
nevertheless, the names Adam and Beatrice, once given,
cannot simply slough off their associations of Man as
Everyman, originally sinful, and Woman as poetic, mythic
love-object.[32] Anyway, such connotations *do* interact with
other, internal pointers to universality, including for example
the typifying of "all women" [46] and of "a girl . . . what a
woman in the making she was." [48] And the similarities
between this particular affair and the couple's own earlier
experiences multiplies the instances of failure, again implying universality. There is nothing that will or choice or
hope can achieve to alter the cycle of mutual destruction,
the seeds of failure being self-perpetuating in the participants.
One failure breeds another because it taints and disables.
Adam cries, "BECAUSE YOU NEVER RECOVER, NEVER." [5]
He even traces back this predetermination to his teenage
betrayal of a childhood sweetheart: "For that one terrible
act of betrayal I have paid and wrecked my once and only
life with every act and decision I've ever made." [48]
One false step is inexpiable and forever destructive.

In the absence of any subsidiary plotting, of other characters, inessential incidents or any other elaborative illustrations of this stark main theme, added resonance can come
only from the two characters' reminiscences of their former
lives, and these reminiscences almost exclusively concern
previous failed love affairs and other partners—lost lover,
betrayed husband or wife. How far the present affair is
repeating the pattern of others we learn partly through this

E

direct reminiscence, partly by implication. At the beginning, hints of a pre-ordained development prepare for what turn out to be actual correspondences. "And now," says Adam, "because there is neither wife nor mistress I sing to you, speak poetry to you. . . ." [7–8] His epithet for Beatrice, a "rare woman", is not new. "So many people have once considered me a rare woman," she replies. [9] Particularly as they quarrel, Adam notices that "You sound like *her*." [52] And just as Adam's answer to Beatrice's remarks is characteristic of a former lover, "just what he would have asked", so Adam's perception that "I know him and I know you and I know all that passed between you," [14] is based on his own familiarity with his role.

Even more explicitly, Adam's former mistress grew, he says, to resent his laughter: and later Beatrice confesses, "I can't bear your laughter, it's unnatural. It casts everybody out." [46] Adam's first woman, guilty of damaging their relationship, would cry for her self-inflicted wounds— whilst of Beatrice's tears of remorse after a quarrel, he says "You cry for yourself." [54] Finally, before the two characters separate for ever, they recall the passing of love, and it does not matter whether the "him" and "her" they regret are their present or former lovers, so indistinguishable have they become.[33] [56–7]

Because the unmodifiable motives for their actions are wholly within the characters—for neither fate nor other people have influenced them—it does not, in this sense, matter who the "other" partner is at any given moment. Neither character is reacting to a particular "other", in fact, but *re-enacting* compulsively what has been dictated by the past. The play is not, therefore, the interaction it at first seems, but rather a pair of parallel actions, inevitably sterile. Adam and Beatrice are mirrors of each other's pain, but as incapable of helping each other as two images behind glass. Adam recognises this, only to forget it later: "We don't really know each other. Even though I look at you and see myself and try to guess yet—I don't know." [5] He has detected the prototype of this bedevilling sterility in his former mistress's passion—"a passion no part of which relates to any living man nor any living man could share". [31] And he tells Beatrice as she quarrels, "You hear what you want to hear, you understand what you need to understand" [34]—which is true of his own underlying self-immersion as well as hers, as the couple go through the gestures of response. The memories of other love affairs deflect real communication, as in Beatrice's retrospective anger, checked by Adam's comment, "You're not talking to *me*, Beatrice," [15] and in his lapse into inconsolable longing for his former mistress, suddenly discounting Beatrice altogether.

In effect, the activating need that both acknowledge— "You need to believe," says Adam, and Beatrice agrees, whilst "I need to be believed" [16]—never generates any new, independent contact. Each character is shut off from sensitivity and responsiveness towards the other's needs by a preoccupation with their own—hence Adam's slighting rebuff to Beatrice's advances, and his preference for truth over reassurance. As Beatrice comments, "To believe in the nonsense of honesty, how wrong you are." [40] And at the end of the play there is a half-truth in her conclusion that "nothing happened. It was all play-acting." [56] What did happen, another convulsion in the inward-turned struggle for happiness, was not the relationship they thought it to be.

The Four Seasons, then, although Wesker calls it "a story about love coming and dying",[34] is not a play about love but a play about jealousy: jealousy pervades it and the gestures of love are pushed into odd corners of the action. The essence of a loving relationship, as the characters recognise, is trust, total commitment, the dropping of all reservations and all barriers—the deepest involvement, and consequently the deepest vulnerability. "Nothing should be held back, ever," says Beatrice. [22] The implications of such total commitment, self-exposure, and dependence within a relationship are pursued further in Adam's earlier belief that "to know more than one person was to betray them". [7] This follows convincingly: to find the partner offering comparable or greater affection and attention to another naturally causes feelings of inadequacy and rejection, connected hurtfully with the most intimate depths of being.

Now this means that the jealousy exposed in the play is a jealousy of the mind: the betrayal in question is of all the aspects of love that transcend or extend the physical. So whenever such jealousy has broken out during former love affairs, or between Adam and Beatrice here and now, a high emotional charge accompanies confessions of the mind's involvement in this betrayal. References to the rival's beauty, power and sexual attractions generally invoke a neutral response. Thus, Beatrice does not interrupt or refer back to Adam's praise of another woman, who "was so endowed with her own loveliness, her own intelligence", [31] but she recoils from the longing and affinity his mind feels for her: "You see things wanting her to see them, you think thoughts wanting her to share them." [34] For this pair, not only is knowing more than one person a betrayal, as in Adam's previous unsuccessful compartmentalising of mistress and wife, but equally having known another, even long before. Again, the irrevocable passing of time prevents the renewal of hope:

Oh, if we had met before we'd been touched by anyone else, you and I. You, Adam, and I—what would we have done together? What wouldn't we have done together! [38]

Each of the three typical affairs the play examines—those of Adam and Beatrice, and of each with a previous lover— has been wrecked by the destructive jealousy of the woman. Jealousy seems to be dramatised by Wesker as a distinctively feminine fault, as the accusation "why does a woman destroy her love with such a desperate possessiveness, why?" [32] and this later, more explicit exchange, both suggest:

BEATRICE: You think me capable of abuse?
ADAM: All women.
BEATRICE: But me? Me? Capable of abuse?
ADAM: All women. [46]

All the generalisations about women assume the truth of this. It is implied in the ironic eulogy of "what a woman in the making she was" already mentioned: and Beatrice as love-object endows herself, truthfully or in symbolic fantasy, with a conventionally feminine, complementary life-style:

Men come to me with their ideas, politicians with their doubts, poets ask my praise. My home is filled with people seeking comfort because they know my instinct is right. [18]

The leisure and vacancy of spirit which breeds obsessive jealousy belongs to this image: that the Beatrice we see could ever have been a forestry-worker, as she says, becomes incongruous, even incredible.

The betrayals perpetrated by Adam, the results of his unwilling attempts at commitment to one person or another —which always involve the exclusion of a third to the injury of all three—form a more delicate, less fully developed variation on the theme, overshadowed by Beatrice's whole-hearted, histrionic jealousy. And perhaps accusations of bareness against *The Four Seasons* have some grounds in this one-sided simplification. In his other plays Wesker's strength lies in a comprehensive and subtle dramatisation of complexity. Complexity does not *have* to be attended by proliferating detail—but here, having dispensed with solidity of environment and all but two characters, Wesker is trying for a forced simplicity by apparently balancing two equally strong personalities, whilst in reality he allows one to overshadow the other, in dramatic substance and "significance" alike.

A related problem is that the action clothes the skeleton of the play inadequately. Adam and Beatrice's one-year relationship has to be developed in words rather than actions, but the words in fact seldom create a sense of originally-felt experience. Methods must of course vary with the aims of the writer, but the archetypally bare plays of Beckett achieve great solidity either by recreating a past in its entirety, as in *Happy Days*, or by obsessively inflating tiny incidents and fantasies into a carefully structured sequence, weaving the rhythmic patterns of life before the audience, with a minimum of supplementary reminiscence, as in *Waiting for Godot*. In *The Four Seasons*, the enacted experiences that form the living-out of the relationship tend to occur in isolated patches—the hair-brushing, the singing lesson, the strudel-making—and the word-flow otherwise keeps returning to recollection, to projected images of former relationships.[35]

These remembered relationships are by comparison so much more solid than the reality—although this is *not*, as in *Happy Days*, the dramatist's object—because they are shaped by incidents well anchored in a realised context. But the physical setting of *The Four Seasons* is not successful in giving its own, present-tense action an appropriate context —although other, comparable works have had symbolic settings, from *Godot*'s swamp and *Play*'s urns to the infernal second-empire drawing-room in *Huis Clos*, that *do* have relevance to their similarly suspended characters. The equivalent in *The Four Seasons*—the neglected house's sad antiques and hand-assembled furniture [1]—is oddly distinct from characters who are both divorced from and doomed by their pasts (unless one conceives it as in deliberate contrast, negatively manifesting the impossibility of escape). And the changes of light and of décor with the seasons are superficial, scarcely more revealing about Adam and Beatrice than they are original in conception.

The abstraction of the relationship into an isolated world is nevertheless connected in intention with the extreme distinction Wesker is making between remediable and ir-remediable evils: individual anguish cannot necessarily be avoided or cured by social adjustments. In Ionesco's *The Killer*, a Radiant City becomes a beautiful setting for death: similarly, Wesker's point is that "even when Jerusalem is built friends will grow apart and mothers will mourn their sons growing old". [56] As Adam says, "the heart has its private aches. You must allow the heart its private aches. Not all the good great causes in this world can stop me crying for a passing love." [56]

Because the relationship with Beatrice, unlike those re-membered, is enacted archetypally, and because its points of reference are symbolic and universal, it is hard for the few episodes of shared experience to strike the casual, *accidentally* typical note necessary to suggest a normal, continuing state. There are no "free scenes", for example, like the "warm hut" episode in *Chips*. Such scenes here keep sinking under the weight of an implied special significance, and obviously a relationship made up only of specially significant moments has no stable identity.

One symbol that does successfully help sum up the play, however, is the guy-scarecrow figure set up as the action draws to an end: this, not the insipid furniture, reflects and

mocks the two characters, who respond to its own unrespon-
siveness with contrasting feelings. To Beatrice it represents
the pretence of response to passions that are always in fact self-
sustained and unrequited: to Adam the pretence is equally
plain and chilling, but at the same time it tempts him to
renounce the more hurtful pretences of human beings. The
scarecrow effectively images his own and Beatrice's in-
communicative monologues of passion, earlier and prophetically called "waxwork passion", [52] and both recognise
this. On the other hand, a non-explicit symbol, like Beatrice's
inability to sing, is quite as effective, because of its veiled
portentousness, warning perhaps of a corresponding harshness, lack of joy or generosity. And, overlapping the line
between verbal and concrete symbol, Adam's song in the
Winter section [6] is another non-specific correlative for the
melancholy of the whole play, a reflection of "sadness and
waste and neglect and suffering". [57]

The verbal images often have ritual or mythic connotations
in keeping with the play's formality, and it is this that elevates
the atmosphere above that of common experience. Beatrice
says "I have a golden eagle for a lover," [29] and she
imagines Adam and herself making carefully patterned plans
for the future, "like schemers of a great ball". [39] Her visions
of their shared life are vast and undomestic in scale: they
would have

> burned paths of sweet-smelling flowers across the world,
> and gone looking in all its curious corners, raised storms
> among the dead. [38]

In the twice repeated phrase of her lover, she is called "a
queen without a country". [14, 38] And her lover, she says,
was a "leader of men", a god. [14] Having para-quoted,
"consider the *Convalaria majalis* how they grow, they toil not,

neither do they spin", [29] a few speeches later, she says, in similarly solemn explication:

> When you need me to be your sun, I'm your sun. When you need soft winds I shall cover the land with my breath. When you need comfort then I shall offer my breasts and my limbs and my lips. [29–30]

Reiterating an imagery that runs through the play, Adam's next long reminiscence warns of "the woman whose love is an oppressive sun". [31] Towards the end of the Spring section Adam responds to Beatrice's "tender and sacrificial" gesture of drawing together their naked breasts by saying "My skin breathes. There is blood flowing through my veins again. My skin breathes." [22] And Beatrice opens the Summer section following with exactly the same words. One image could even be said to link, by analogy at least, the pathos of the characters' crippled lives with the neglected, sad furniture, as, here, Beatrice ponders on the divergence between her underlying aspirations and her perverse behaviour:

> I'm ashamed of my worn limbs, second-hand. Third-hand to be precise; third-hand bruised and damaged— like a clock striking midnight when the hour is only six, and it wheezes and whirs. But the hands always point to the right time. And if we had met each other before we had met anyone else then the hands would have pointed to the right time and the right hour would have sung clear and ringing. [38]

Like the authenticity of his dialect, the poetry of Wesker's dialogue depends heavily on the shape imposed by rhythm. This is usually unobtrusive, just marked by a repeated word, as "safe" links the opening triple and single sentences of the first section: "We're safe, it's all right, no one lives here. You don't think anywhere is safe, do you?" [1] Adam similarly expands sentences out of single words: "Warm. The first thing, always, is to be warm." Or "Invalid. You are an invalid, aren't you?" [2] And he abstracts words from phrases: "Such a lovely face. A face I could love. Even 'love' again." [2] Then, in a long speech, such as Beatrice's soliloquy while Adam is ill, there is perfect control over the continuous prose. Even a comparatively short passage is held together by this control:

> Peace, majesty and great courage—never. I've found none of these things. Such bitter disappointment. Bitter. Bitter, bitter, bitter. And out of such bitterness cruelty grows. You cannot understand the cruelty that grows. And I meant none of it, not one cruel word of it. And he knew and I knew and we both knew that we knew, yet the cruelty went on. [39]

Gradually and musically Beatrice's thought unfolds, in the step-by-step progression of "bitter . . . bitterness . . . cruelty . . . . . . cruel," and so on. And the movement varies from the slowness of the simple opening statements, with their pauses on "never" and "bitter", through the acceleration of "Bitter, bitter, bitter", to the more rapid sentences, lightly punctuated and without pauses at the close of the passage.

In the soliloquy of which this forms a part, small patterns resolve themselves into Beatrice's refrain of "peace, majesty and great courage". And this refrain is first foreshadowed, in foreshortened form, in the earlier assertion, "All my life I have looked for peace and majesty, for a man. . . ." [38] The tact and sensitivity of fine prose writing demand that repetition should not be laboured or mechanical, and Wesker allows this refrain to emerge on just two more occasions before concluding with the weightier variation: "And peace, above all—peace, and trust and majesty and all that great courage." [39]

Beatrice tends throughout the play to use more extended, expansive sentences than Adam. The couple share a standard syntax and vocabulary, and differentiation between them is, accordingly, not spectacular: but as a rule Adam's style leans towards jerkiness, or at least abruptness, in his strings of short sentences or in the longer sentences chopped up into successive "and . . . and . . . and" sections. However, Adam is slightly more original in the purposefully chosen words he uses, whereas Beatrice falls back quite often on ready-made phrases, usually of a conventionally sophisticated middle-class kind. For example, when Adam speaks of "a terrible, terrible precision", [48] he really means to convey a sense of terror: but when Beatrice says, "Oh we're awful creatures all right," [21] she is using "awful" in its slack and imprecise sense, as a generally denigratory label. Class-oriented responses, verbal and emotional, also help to round out her character in conversational tags like "You're very sweet, but—" [19] and "I'm a bore, aren't I?" [15] In short, the language of the play is not a homogeneous, merely functional continuum: for Wesker does not need pronounced contrasts of character type or the resources of unfamiliar dialect to distinguish language styles, but, as in *The Friends*, delicately separates different characters with basically similar speech patterns.

With *The Four Seasons* Wesker's style had thus expanded to achieve an expressive and compelling poetry, embryonic in the flexibility and allusiveness of *Chips*. Structurally the play is only half-successful: the cyclical form certainly suits the theme of recurrence and inevitability, but the external framework of the four seasons is also constraining, an artificial imposition. The impression of rigidity probably derives

from the way lighting, costumes and décor are all too obed-
ient to their appropriate seasons, the action itself developing
afterwards in conformity instead of *generating* the changes of
seasonal atmosphere. And, for a play that sets out to trace
the blossoming and withering of a love affair, *The Four
Seasons* tends too much to neglect its own action in order to
refer back to former relationships. There just isn't enough
happening on stage and needing expression to limit the overwhelming reminiscences by natural means.

It is interesting to note that Wesker's concern with private
pain should have been dramatised in *The Four Seasons*,
while in *Golden City*, begun earlier but written concurrently,
he should have concentrated on the interaction of social and
personal ethics. For Andrew Cobham was caught up in
problems that were strangely similar to Adam's: he too
excluded his wife from his world of ideas, so as to heighten
his compatibility with Kate, but the tenor of their personal
relationship had mainly to be deduced from their public
behaviour. This emphasis is obviously in complete contrast
to that of *The Four Seasons*: indeed, one of Wesker's dominating themes in *Golden City* had been the inescapable influence
of public action—not emotional encounters—on the powers
of feeling. But in his next play, *The Friends*, first staged in
London at the Round House on 19th May 1970, he was to
attempt a much more fully satisfying realisation of private
pain without over-emphasising or amputating his characters'
more diffuse everyday experiences.

The Friends is an almost indigestibly rich play, the more so
because its development is not articulated step by episodic
step, like that of *Golden City*, or symbolically symmetrical,
like that of *The Four Seasons*: instead, the condensed and
involuted substance of the action is packed into a successive
afternoon, night and morning, a period of less than twenty-
four hours. The six friends of the title are designers of

"twentieth-century interiors", owners of a small chain of
shops that market their ideas: and the only other character,
the eldest, is Mr Mason, familiarly Macey, the manager of the
biggest store. During the play, all are assembled in the room of
Esther, the dominant character, who is dying of leukaemia.

The play has, unexpectedly, strong thematic similarities
to John Osborne's *Hotel in Amsterdam*—though it differs
significantly from it in form. Written at about the same time
and at the same stage of its author's career, Osborne's play
too is concerned with a gathering of six friends on the brink
of middle-age. But Osborne's characters are, in spite of
various dissatisfactions and some controlled tension, adjusted
to their stable lives and especially to each other—they are
comfortable together. And they are dominated by an off-
stage boss, of whose unexpected suicide they learn only at the
end of the play, the curtain thus falling on a note of sudden
uncertainty. Here, on the contrary, Esther's death exactly
half-way through *The Friends* crucially focuses the feelings
of disorientation, despair, fear and threatened paralysis
that have been infecting the other characters during the
advance of her own physical illness. The group threatens to
founder and fall apart when Esther, a strong influence to the
end, ceases to draw its members together: but from this sense
of disequilibrium, the characters progress to a painful
readjustment to living. First, however, they have to come to
terms with their own burdens of experience and self-
knowledge, and with the process of ageing that is now both
limiting the possibilities of their lives, and bringing nearer the
reality of death that has already claimed Esther. The
attempt to deal with this rising tide of amorphous, choking
doubt, to force a meaningful shape upon the external and
internal void into which life seems crumbling, is the absorbing concern of the characters and of the play.

This concern resolves itself into a dual preoccupation with

death and with the senseless fragmentation of the world, including the friends' own past lives. Esther, who knows she is dying, is in love with life, but the others are transfixed by horror or helplessness as they contemplate their pasts, what they are, what faces them. Each has his or her own fund of inadequacies, with which to augment the common consciousness of failure. Roland, Esther's lover, was once, according to Macey, a "brilliant man, brilliant! Figures were games for him." [28] Now an existential terror oppresses him. He slips into catatonic panic after Esther's death:

> That tight brain I had, all wrapped up with confidence—it's fallen apart. Everything I love I don't feel for now. What do I do? [56]

Instead of using this brain, he now desperately seeks and lays hold of systems. Macey: "He wants to become an aesthete! Once he wanted to be a voluptuary. From one extreme to another." [28] He acts out personal rituals, like yoga contemplation and self-inflicted razor wounds, in the hope of thereby miraculously subduing his sense of oppression; and the gashes that he rubs with salt, in an attempt to share and diminish Esther's pain, stand out only more shockingly than his other adopted postures, as products of a random, irrational, superstitiously gesturing mind.

Esther describes Manfred, her brother, as "a gentle person". He has not abandoned a humanistic approach to experience, which he rationalises with a desperate attempt at understanding, so that even "other people's need to hate makes such sense to him". [46] But Crispin, another of the friends, accuses:

> He doesn't find the world strange. Only lovely and interesting. Explanations for everybody, no evil for him. Lovely compassions and tender opinions he has. [17]

Manfred, however, is finding his rational approach itself fragmentary in form and effect: it can be applied to this or that problem but does not *relate* one small area of understanding to another. He recognises this:

> Do you know, new knowledge disrupts me. Because there's no solid rock of learning in this thin, undernourished brain of mine, so each fresh discovery of a fact or an idea doesn't replace, it undermines the last. [18]

So Crispin's objection that Manfred ignores the existence of evil is not quite true: he admits it—but does not let it connect with experience.

And no more than Roland is he integrated or at peace within himself. His explanations do not affect his feelings: his understanding of the need of others to hate is intellectual and quite detached from his own emotions. Therefore, in spite of his superficial tolerance, by the end of act one he has confessed that he despises "the Englishman" [35] and hates the working class. Hate bursts through a veneer of reasoned principles with disruptive force, a disruption akin to that suffered by Ronnie, aware of the disintegration of his communist faith, in *Chicken Soup*, or, indeed, akin to the socialist Christopher's in Cecil Taylor's *Allergy*, or to the anarchist Hugo's in *The Iceman Cometh*—all spectacularly dramatic twists of plot. But in this play Manfred's outbursts are firmly linked to the central theme, because they are part of the whole pattern (paradoxically) of disintegration and insecurity that is afflicting the friends.

It is, however, the impact of emotional not intellectual discords that attacks Crispin. The "problem of evil" occupies him—evil as a "willingness to do a thing which is the opposite of goodness. A *willingness*, a love, an active willingness. Evil!" [17–18] And it occupies him particularly in the form of sadism: helplessly he absorbs it into his own personality, cruelly provoking Manfred and Simone, the only one of the friends of upper-class origins, who loves Crispin and, in so doing, embarrasses him. She, like Manfred, has to protest: "Talk to *me*, Crispin. I've got a name, I'm in the room." [61] And their protests point to what Crispin is doing: dismissing in his oblique, third-person comments, directed *at* them not *to* them, their humanity and capacity for response. He does not rationalise, but reacts with aggression or fear: "Everything terrifies me. Babies, dogs, flies, lightning." [11] He fends off, more or less brutally, the affectionate attentions of Simone: he wants reciprocated love, but because he is drawn by some strange desire or need into brief affairs with old women, his tenderness is spent in the guilt and the turbulent, again ambivalent sensations of these involvements.

And there's shame and disgust and pleasure and it's all consumed me. Unnatural passions! They take out guts from a man. . . . And I've destroyed mesen I have; offended and confused the soul, see? [58]

The self-conscious reversion to dialect hides the shame and the seriousness of the confession.

The fears of Tessa, the most extrovert of the friends, are mainly associated with ageing. "We're none of us what we thought we were," she repeats; [57, 61] and she complains of having bunions, of growing old, and, more than the others, of feeling "cluttered"—"trapped" by the past. Her assumed persona—one of self-possessed, slightly comic fury—has engrained itself into a habit, grafted to her personality like a pirandellian mask: and her reaction is to strive to cut away and throw off all the overwhelming clutter of memories and custom that she can do nothing with. As for Simone, cut off by her upper-class upbringing from the early shared experiences of the others, it is never made clear how long her suffering has gone on, though it is apparently of much longer standing than Esther's illness. And the "stillness" Macey comments on seems to be as habitual to her as anger to Tessa:

> Everyone tells me that. It's not stillness really, it's fear. A protective silence. If I say too much or do too much I'm always afraid someone'll stamp on me. I feel so raw most of the time, such a useless human being. [33]

Simone's problem is that she has a governing need to belong and to be wanted, but has joined a group in which she is bound to be the odd one out—the only upper-class southerner among five working-class art college friends from the "same warm northern city". She is "so desperate to be wanted. I'd do anything for that." [33] But the need is somehow self-defeating, inviting rejection, over-obvious, too demanding, too embarrassing. She is not strong or confident enough to stand alone, so that the conviction of her own inadequacy makes life oppressive to her. "It all defeats me," she confesses—and, repulsed on every side, unable to make contact, Simone more than the others finds herself in a situation approaching an absurdist isolation:

> You don't know what it's like to talk and not be heard; to offer and not be taken; to be full and not needed. There's not a creature needs me, not one single one. They'll use me, drink with me, tolerate my company but not need—not really need me. And I feel so useless and rejected, so dismissed. You've never known that, have you? God's chosen ones you lot are, but not me. [52]

Simone, the rejected one, and Macey, on the periphery

of the group, are both outsiders: and this affinity enables
them, at the end of the play, to survey the friends and their
accumulation of fears from an involved yet objective viewpoint. Thus, they offer an assessment and redirection that
have nothing to do with the more inwardly-circling recrim-
inations and quarrels. Simone's suffering derives quite as
much from the failings of those who respond to her as from
her own, and her adjustment to the fragments and patches of
experience that paralyse the others is already accomplished:
but she cannot make use of this adjustment while her solitary
misery cuts her off—like Esther, against her will—from the
life of the others.

Macey's position is if anything more complicated than
Simone's, though not dissimilar. He has ordered his priorities,
he can cope with what happens to him, he can distinguish
his own deficiences from the world's impositions and see
how each stands in relation to the other:

But the next discipline was really hard, you listening,
Roland? Really hard! It was to avoid building up those
little heavyweight philosophies about man and the
world out of my own personal disappointments; to avoid
confusing self-hatred with hatred of all men; to face the
fact that though I'd failed, others hadn't. [55]

So Macey is not at the mercy of emotional reactions, as
Tessa is, nor of disruptive surprises about his own inconsistent beliefs and feelings, as is Manfred. Instead, like Simone,
his life is sapped by the failure of a personal relationship—
with his wife. This can be accepted but not ignored:

Because each morning I wake up knowing that I don't love
the woman at my side, and haven't done so for the last
fifteen years—That defeats me that does, that really does

defeat me. No love—no appetites, for nothing. Even before the day begins I'm done. [54]

In explanation of this defeat, Macey recalls that at one time she had been all he wished for, a measure of himself, and so: "I resent her because she makes me despise myself. She reminds me, every day, that at one time in my life I'd wanted such small things." [55] But this is less convincing: such persistent contempt for a past self seems oddly superfluous.

Like Manfred, Macey ends his apologia for his restraint and resentment by admitting no efficacy to the making of admissions:

But who's satisfied? No one is—are they? Because they're no good really, those little bits of honest confession. What am I supposed to do with them, tell me what? [55]

As in Simone's case his lack of fulfilment is due not to any maladjustment to universal complexities—problems like purpose, ageing, death—but to a special set of conditions, an externally imposed emotional burden. Yet, paradoxically, his own and Simone's *private* pain is less subjective in source than the rest of the group's, and therefore less responsive to their own understanding.

These several inabilities to see meaning in particular facets of existence unite in the friends' symptomatic and seminal disillusionment with their work, the designing and selling that, by creating and propagating beauty, was to have been their contribution to regenerating society, and thus to have given purpose to their own lives. Simone and Macey discuss how the other five built their shops with their "labouring fathers and tight-lipped mothers" in mind: but neither they nor anyone like them came to the shops—only the middle class pseudo-intelligentsia who proved unresponsive to proselytising aesthetic education. [33–4] Macey's remarks about the friends' tendencies to excess [27] serve as a measure of their original aspirations too: now they are disgusted with the failure of their plan and, sour-grapes fashion, with its inevitable patchiness. The imminent, literal bankruptcy of the shops is the bankruptcy of their vision—typically, of their inability to relate—and their reaction in this disgust is to cut themselves off completely from the shops and all the clutter of the past that these represent.

Now that this absorbing sense of purpose has evaporated, they find, disenchanted, that they have grown older. The fear of ageing links their disorientation with a more primitive fear of death: on all sides they are trapped—by a wasted past; by a present that is a confusion of meaningless details, and that, in its meaninglessness, offers no reason for choosing any goal or line of action; and by a future that is in any case menacingly shortening before them, at once making the *use* of their lives a matter of urgency, and limiting the possibilities of usefulness open to them. This adds to the feeling of oppression, as Manfred explains:

We're growing old bit by bit. Every word is a second, passing. It'll never return, never. That's so absolute. I shall never be young again. I shall never laugh the same way again, I shall never love for the first time again, never discover my first sight of the sea, nor climb my first mountain, nor stumble across literature, never; I'll reach out to recapture or remember—but the first ecstasy of all things? Never again. [35]

Esther's death lies at the centre of the play in more ways than one. If the friends' *ad hoc* philosophies warp and fracture before the onslaught of the contradictions of reality, they crumble utterly before the fact of death. As one of their number, Esther in dying forces upon them this ultimate reality—the time when "the commonplace 'We must all die' transforms itself suddenly into the acute consciousness 'I must die—and soon.' "[36] And their reactions range from Tessa's despair of anything "left worth the while to do" [59] to Roland's cult-following attempts at masochistic self-discipline. The earlier incapacities are aggravated to the point of crisis.

All these fears, from Manfred's sense of philosophic imbalance to Roland's primitive terror, develop organically out of the thematic movement of the play. The friends have no way of responding to Esther's death because of their general, group-disintegration. A society that has a unified world-picture—that senses such a total meaning in the universe as (for example) the traditionally assured vision of medieval christendom—grants its members a frame of reference which cannot only contain a purpose for living, but also make possible the acceptance of death. This can be just as true of smaller groups, or of individuals: but here the company of friends cannot come to terms with life—it has been unable to disentangle such a meaningful pattern from the chaos of the universe it perceives.

Even acceptance of death need not, however, imply willingness to die—especially not at an early age. As Esther asks: "Do you know anybody who was prepared to die? Despite all the suffering and the knowledge of suffering and man's inhumanity everyone wants to go on living— for ever and ever, gloriously." [31] Esther's death represents archetypal Death so fully just because she has been so fully representative of life. Thus, it was unnecessary to add comment upon Esther's insecurities in discussing those of the other six: for she alone had sensed no threat or void in her life, except having to leave it. As Macey tells Roland later: "You're weird, all of you. And unnatural. Esther was the only healthy one of the lot of you." [53] Her struggle against death is natural. And whereas Roland's fear of the miserable loss of will death inflicts on the others is entirely negative, Esther logically resents death because she finds life good—she positively wants to live:

I can't tell you how much I cherish everything. I know there's a lot that's obscene and ugly but it's never been too oppressive, I've always had the capacity not to be oppressed. *You* know that, don't you, Roland? In the end there's such sweetness, such joy in hidden places. I want to stay on and not miss anything. I want to stay with you, all of you, close and warm and happy. Why shouldn't I want that? [32]

But although willingness to die is neither easy nor desirable, the acceptance of death that means simply withstanding the prospect of its inevitability—the capacity not to be oppressed by the concept, not to allow it to spread like a slow stain over the rest of life—is what the surviving friends have yet to learn. Salvation lies through Esther, because, without imposing upon herself the rigidity of a religious or philosophic ethic, her joy in life, her ability to receive and enjoy or subdue every successive impression, amounts in effect to the necessary coherent view of life, a means of assimilating and assessing the chaos of the external world. Her resilience, her power of enjoying what comes, her refusal to be crushed by inhumanity and ugliness, must be inherited by her survivors if they are to go on, so that they can "place" death among those sufferings and obscenities that hurt but do not overwhelm. In Esther, the pain of death has affirmed the value of life.

So, through Esther's death, the other characters are led back to life. In the last scene Simone tells them finally what

she has always known, that deciding on and trusting a scale
of values—which has to be absolute, not shifting or relative,
even if concerned with beauty, the beauty of an antique
chair—is the way to judge the confusion of life. And judgement is the longed-for way to transform confusion into order
—order, the meaningful pattern that cannot be managed
without, as Macey reminds them: "Well you haven't earned
the right to anarchy yet. You've created confusion and chaos
and the habit of discontent and you haven't earned the
right." [65] Through values and judgement, good remains
stably good and is not superceded, as are Manfred's random,
unselected slivers of knowledge, by the awareness of what is
evil. Simone adds: "And what's more—there's room for
failure when you've got order, and for weaknesses and—
and—" Crispin interposes: "For everyman's fallibility?" [65]

Here, climactically, the diverse thematic threads of the
play are drawn together. Tessa confronts Simone's solution
with the friends' fears of death and ageing:

But she's talking about order and nobility and Esther's
lying there dead and it's all irrelevant. Look at this room,
look at the lovely order we've cluttered ourselves with.
Dead and ancient riches, PERFECT . . . ! And now we're
trapped, hung up by it all. Bits and pieces of us all over the
place. [66]

And, more gently, Manfred describes their discouragement
and exhaustion:

Our mess is not only made of Esther's dying but the
knowledge that this is a once and only life more than half
over and if you want to thrash the gloom from us then
you'd have to give us back youth and the strength not to
despise ourselves. Not all your haranguing us to order

political priorities can clear up such a mess as that. It
can't be ignored, that one, not that one. [69–70]

Esther herself has been the living refutation of all these
arguments. Loving all sensations, especially ancient and rich
ones, and armed with a sense of discrimination that did not
only order *political* priorities, she was passionately in love
with life, yet as old—or as young—as the rest of the friends.

In a final, bizarre and powerful sequence, Simone uses
Esther's body to make the group realise the testimony of her
life. Repeating "*she* wanted to live . . . she wanted to *live* . . .
she wanted to live", [70] she raises the body to a chair,
helped by Roland, and gradually, without speaking, the
others relax, the sense of oppressive gloom slipping away as
the memories and happiness they have known together,
especially with Esther, reassert their value, and death, age
and fragmentation loosen their nightmarish hold on the
play. The closing stage direction reads:

Thus seated, the others are forced to accept the presence
of the dead among them. Slowly they relax and one by one
kiss her cheek, then—
Manfred returns to his model; Tessa and Crispin go
to the bed to fold away the blankets; Roland sits by
Esther as though guarding her. Simone begins to clear
away coffee cups and dirty ashtrays. Macey watches them
a while, reaches for his jacket, half leaves, turns to smile
at Roland, returns to kiss Esther, leaves—
—and a slow, slow fading away. [71]

In deeds rather than words, and so without intellectualising
their readjustment, the friends are beginning to accept
Esther's way, reconciled to what life has offered to them.

A degree of complexity is inevitable in the development of

this theme towards its final resolution, since no less than seven characters of major importance are directly caught up in the action: but the complexity is not due merely to the seven facets the problem is thus given. If the play's subject is definable crudely as the attempt to find order in mutiplicity, then everywhere its density reproduces this multiplicity— the action of the play perfectly predicates its theme. The richness of texture in dialogue and action works against the recurrent wish to cut off from the past and its "clutter", to deny what experience and age have added to individuality, and to start again from the blank slate of youthfulness.

This assertive richness is realised, too, in the set, the room that is the result and the correlative of the friends' lives. Tessa's revulsion against the room is thus connected with her rejection of age and attendant experience:

> I can't bear this room any more. We've built too much of ourselves into it. Singing, plotting, loving—such a lot to be remembered, arrangements, smells, odd bargains— all that spent love and devotion—too rich, too too rich. [66]

Yet the room contains not only representations of the friends' own experiences, but objects of experience from the still further distant past—and this Crispin finds incongruous:

> Dishonest that's what it is. We own five shops selling twentieth-century interiors which we've designed, *we've* designed mind you, and yet look at this room. Bits and pieces from other men's decades. [15]

It is a two-hundred-year-old chair that Tessa overthrows as an expression of her hatred of the room that is an image of all their lives: but the room is nominally—and rightfully—

Esther's. Rightfully, because she has been able to cope with its multiplicity, whether this mirrors the accumulated experience of herself or of the friends.

The importance of accumulated experience thus nourishing the spirit is stressed in much of Wesker's thinking. In a lecture he has defined the true artist as a man who is able to assimilate all that has been passed on to him, and who understands:

> not that he is a man of our time, but that he is a man at the
> end of a long line of all time; not that he uses twentieth-
> century eyes, but that he uses twenty centuries of man's
> accumulated sensibilities and experience. The true artist
> knows that the past is too rich with endeavour, suffering,
> and achievement to be dismissed and ignored.[37]

And so Simone leaps to restore the overturned chair "lovingly", protesting: "You should love it. . . . Memory, the past, signs of human activity—you should cherish them— I adore this room." [66] Significantly, then, the evocative force of her environment sustains and reinforces Esther's own earlier statement of her beliefs, with its verbal echo of Wesker's:

> My brother's a rebel, Macey, I—am a revolutionary. He
> talks about leaders of our time, I see a need for men who
> belong to the end of a long line of all time. He's obsessed
> with our responsibility to the twentieth century, I'm
> obsessed with our responsibility to an accumulation of
> twenty centuries of sensibility. My brother is a rebel
> because he hates the past, I'm a revolutionary because I
> see the past as too rich with human suffering and achieve-
> ment to be dismissed. Women are natural revolutionaries,
> aren't they, Simone? Men are only ever rebels, their angers
> are negative, tiny. [46]

The Friends, at the time of writing furthest of Wesker's plays from *The Kitchen*, is thus complementary to his earliest work, dealing with exactly the opposite area of experience. In the kitchen there was nothing but work, no time to develop or to make friends: here, there is friendship and shared development upon which work has been dependent, until what has been increasingly, albeit unconsciously, shaping the friends' lives, begins to exclude work altogether. In the accumulated clutter of the room itself, Macey notices the contrast between these increasingly dissonant forces:

> You're all very strange to me in these surroundings. It's so large, this house, and full of other things. Not like the shop at all. Full of light and brightness there, but here— Old Nick lives here. It's too rich. [26]

The richness, as Esther says, represents the past, which is "too rich . . . to be dismissed". And in direct opposition to the room's accumulation of hundreds of years of human sensibility are the shops, selling their assertively twentieth-century interiors, and signifying both the friends' original regenerative social and aesthetic purposes, and the rootlessness of their minds. Thus, the impending bankruptcy spells out not only the failure of a reforming vision, but the insufficiency of a set of incoherent philosophies.

Manfred's compulsive dabbling among the sciences illustrates the theme as it interacts with another discipline. In the fine and applied arts they practice, the friends have sought for "originality", for designs which are not dependent upon a corrupt past: whereas Manfred's self-taught science embraces several centuries, but still achieves no synthesis. Each item of knowledge, however ancient its origin, is for him as baseless and unintegrated as some freshly-minted paradox. Manfred recognises how impossible

it is for his fragmentary knowledge to be beneficial to him—
"it's got no measurement by which to judge itself, no perspective by which to evaluate its truth or its worth" [18]—but,
consistently inconsistent, he does not apply *this* deduction to
his own intellectual and emotional maladjustment.

Manfred, a literary dabbler too, also touches upon the
recurrent theme of communication. He has read that
the coming of print—or "the phonetic alphabet", or
"words", or "reading", for no distinction is made—has
had a dislocating effect on human perception. Macey, whose
genius really lies in words, takes up their defence, not this
time as bridges but as gates: and to Manfred's parrotted
assertion that words are dams he replies that they precede
perception and are guides towards it, offering a hope of
giving "solid shape" to vague impressions, "to what before
was only an intangible feeling. Words dams? They're gates,
precious magnificent—lovely!" [20-2] "Words" represent
all the kinds of communication by which links are perceived
and the enriching potential of the past is transmitted. Denial
of communication corresponds to the chaos of unrelated
experience, and to the isolation that lack of context has
inflicted on the characters.

Thus, Roland's abandonment to floundering panic after
Esther's death is symbolised by his rejection of words. "I
can't find words; and words I find I don't want to use and
words I use I don't believe in." Directs Wesker: "he opens
his mouth to say something and cannot". [56–7] Similarly,
Simone's attempts to communicate with the others always
meet with calm but firm repression, until her isolation makes
her unable to tell them the truths they need, except by using
the sympathetic Macey as intermediary and interpreter.
"Unfortunately her terror of them makes her inaudible. . . ."
[64] An inability to speak is invariably a sign that something is wrong.

On the play's own terms, its communication with its audience is intense: every incident and reference, every line, is suffused with significance. The concern with ageing, for example, lends an ironic importance to every mention of youth. Here, Simone is describing the strangeness of the younger people she meets:

Beautiful boys and girls with long hair and colourful bits and pieces they buy from our shop. All styles—Victorian, art-nouveau, military—as though they're attracted by the pomp and circumstance of traditions they hated—like cats playing with mice before devouring them. And they want only one thing, these people. To love. It's as though they're surrounded by so much ugliness and greed that they have to spend all their time convincing themselves that other things exist. [28]

Macey is less puzzled, more hostile, in his description of these more decorative versions of the "young uns" Stan Mann had despised in *Roots*:

They shift about in personalities that've got nothing to do with them, and they drag around some old cult, and they stick alien feelings on to themselves. . . . All right, so they've got a—a sweet-natured grubbiness, but they're still susceptible to loud-mouthed culture and political fraudulence. They'll never produce anything, not this time round. Have to abandon hope this decade. [29]

But these passages are not just digressions or even side-lights upon creeping feelings of age—though, as Simone says, "what's irritating about the young is that we're not". [29] Rather, their details interlock into the larger pattern of the play. Hatred of tradition, an abstract kind of loving, the attempt to escape from ugliness, cult-hopping, helpless susceptibility to new ideas—all these are mirror-images of the afflictions of the friends themselves. Macey pictures their own youth in just such terms:

> The habit of discontent was all your lot ever created. Making the young feel that the world belonged only to them. Real little class terrorists you were, intimidating everyone over the age of twenty-five with your swinging this and your swinging that. You never thought you'd grow old or die. [53–4]

The glamour and decorative sweetness have gone sour, the "innocent charms" no longer work: [63] but part of the friends' revulsion from age does stem from regret for the crudeness and naïvety of lost youth. The emptiness of that blank page seems preferable to their present muddle of accumulated experience, for the "first ecstasy of all things" that Manfred laments [35] is really a substitute for ordered evaluation, a longing for the time before the need for it was known.

Equally, an abrogation of the responsibility to order experience attaches to those who imitate eternal youth by treating every impression as a strange, new one.

> Some men could, some men could stay perplexed and wondering all their life and still survive. All their life . . . amazed . . . ! Each moment—surprised . . . ! And finally— joyous! Joyous to be witness to it all. [50]

Speciously, this seems to resemble the confident capability to evaluate all impressions that Esther has acquired by quite other means: in truth an irresponsible perplexity, it is only another angle on the viewpoint that has no perspective.

The opening of the very first scene illustrates the allusiveness of Wesker's technique in detail: as at the beginning of *The Three Sisters*, seeming monologues are interspersed and blended together so that each comments on the others. Esther, Manfred and Roland speak alternately, and what they say juxtaposes the relative values governing their lives. Esther returns to what she has tested and found constantly pleasurable and evocative:

> The sound of French, that's beautiful; and Russian icons and pre-Raphaelites and Venetian chandeliers . . . And Baroque churches and houses, fountains and market places and the music of organs and Norman arches and wine and the cooking of friends and the sound of friends. [9–10]

Roland, just awakened, is on the verge of his aesthetic phase, and is busy cataloguing emotional responses: "And because of that long sleep everything about me is sharp and alive. . . . I can isolate sounds and tastes and smells." Manfred is reading compulsively—searching for the eternal, for something that exists independent of the memory or the senses: "The electron is a completely universal fundamental particle. . . . It is stable and long lived. For all practical purposes it is indestructible. . . ." [10] And not only are these alternative approaches to reality revelatory of the speakers and reflective upon each other, but they are profoundly poignant because Esther is dying: the images she values and the common sensory responses now constitute her life, and exist only as long as she does. Not being an eternal, fundamental particle, but merely human, she has to die.

Even the finest details have a resonance that reaches beyond the play. The assembly of the friends on the evening of Esther's death—the event that is to lead them back towards life—thus has its own strain of religious symbolism. Tessa's feet are washed by Simone, an action that as in *Chips* has a symbolic significance, this time for the rejected, humble girl herself: and Macey is invited to share what proves to be Esther's last supper. There are, too, close echoes of *Roots*, the subject of which is so similar. The friends' scattered, incoherent lives have "no, no—majesty", [15] and Tessa asks accusingly, during Simone's concluding, suddenly articulate speech, "The apple doesn't fall far from the tree, does it?" [67] More locally, ironic word-play within one speech effects a serious meaning-shift when Macey is coerced into explaining "why I'm a manager": his personal disillusionment has soured inspiration and creativity, but not sapped his capability—and so, "I've managed. A good father taught me discipline so I managed." [54] But "what kind of life is manage?" The question asked in *The Kitchen* has, as it were, identical professional and practical implications—of the second-best.

. *The Friends* sustains in its dialogue a different mood from the earlier plays which is perhaps closest to that of *The Four Seasons*: intimate, introspective, retrospective, it creates, because of the larger cast, an impression of greater interaction. The friends do know each other very well, and communication—except in the passages of obvious breakdown—must be understood to take place between them with the minimum of outward decoration. As the Chekhovian opening suggests, the play is "conversational": and the conversations proceed tangentially from subject to subject and from character to character, instead of by exhaustive ponderings over specific topics. Often the characters express themselves in monologues that are, as in *Roots* and *Chips*, almost meditations, which may or may not be taken up by another character's response. At the same time the friends share each other's opinions more than they realise. For

example: Crispin and Manfred argue in the first scene about
cruelty, understanding and love, and Crispin mocks at
Manfred's gentleness, asserting the reality of evil. "You still
think we love each other don't you?" [17] Yet by the end of
the third scene he and Manfred have simultaneously conceded what amounts to a reversal of positions. Whilst
Manfred now admits to the poisoning effects of hatred,
Crispin only wants "Peace, silence. Blessed peace and
silence," confessing, "It's true—we must love one another,
or die."[38] [49–50]

Their reciprocal confessions are described by Wesker as "a
contrapuntal duologue between Manfred and Crispin". [47]
And this is reminiscent of the duologue between Pip and
Charles in *Chips*—and, perhaps significantly, Wesker traced
back those characters to two sides of himself. For Crispin
and Manfred can alternate between moral positions because
they are, in origin, equal, unstable sharers of the same
fragmented vision. As in the play's opening sequence, this
duologue comments upon itself: and Manfred's fear of the
"ordinary man's" degeneration into vegetable torpor
breaks up two appeals by Crispin for peace and silence. Their
see-sawing spirits refute one another:

MANFRED: Sad, like disappointed lovers, all that love,
gangrenous, inside us.
CRISPIN: We must just be calm.
MANFRED: I try to ignore it, start afresh, find the world
extraordinary—
CRISPIN: It's true—we must love one another, or die.
MANFRED:—but I've no energy, no appetites for new loves.
[50]

And to this similarity of the play in style to *The Four
Seasons* can be added certain similarities of theme and

F

structure. *The Four Seasons* is about a kind of pain that is un-responsive to external social remedies: and this "private pain", though not in the same form, underpins the action of *The Friends*. Manfred makes the distinction, admitting yet qualifying Simone's charges of a more "social" kind of inadequacy:

> That's not the half of it. Our mess is made of other things, like fears, pretensions and disappointments. It's not made of our confusion about who should own eighteenth-century chairs, it's made of—the silly things we've added to the world: easy achievements, ephemeral success. It's not because we've forgotten about injustices and the pursuit of happiness, it's because of little damages we've done to each other and a terrible sense of defeat and time passing and appetites fading and intellect softening. [69]

Manfred goes on to mourn the passing of their "once and only life", the same phrase that Adam uses in *The Four Seasons*: and this awareness of irreversibility, of limited and ever-diminishing choices, of betrayed hopes, is a particular concern of both plays.

The verses Tessa and the others sing before Esther's death even look back to the turning of the seasons:

> We've buried the winter
> Married the spring,
> And now we have a time to pause
> And think again and sing. [44]

Here there is a looking-forward to growth, a sense of continu-ous renewal—and the song seems, indeed, to emerge almost in spite of itself, a remembrance of things past. Nowhere else in the play is there the feeling of cyclical crisis it reflects—which, in its infinite and ill-fated repetition, underlies the pessimism of *The Four Seasons*. And the neoclassic continuity of *The Friends*—encompassing less than the twenty-four hours which gives *The Kitchen* its suggestion of typicality—suits its subject, a once-for-all crisis that reaches, simultaneously, resolution and a fresh start.

In theme and structure alike, *The Friends* pivots upon the death of Esther. The three scenes of the first act prepare for this shock—and the opening establishment of situation and character is Wesker's most casual exposition, even Esther's illness at first only inferentially understood to be leukaemia. The second scene contains a clear foretaste of despair and disintegration. Manfred brings to the surface his sublimated contempt for his countrymen. Roland burns money. Crispin pours public scorn upon Simone's love, and the letters which inadequately express it. And the scene concludes with a "tableau of misery and silence". [39] Then there is, in contrast, some semblance of the contented communion the friends are capable of achieving, in which even Manfred's depression is balanced by Crispin's new hopefulness. But the lightening of tone is brief and deceptive, and Esther's death strikes at a moment of unprepared relaxation.

The three short scenes that begin the second act witness one individual's hopeless rejection of death. Roland is stripped of dignity, philosophy, even words, in a symbolic descent into annihilation reminiscent of (yet so much more recognisably human than) Bérenger's in Ionesco's *Exit the King*. The battle for survival is fought out in the final scene—and maybe too much is crammed into its relatively short span, for the argument is complex, and the internal logic far from easy to assimilate. But the final, daring sequence, in which Esther's dead body is humbly and hesitantly re-introduced into the action, is simultaneously a brilliant *coup de théâtre* and a confident realignment of attitudes and action, in which the future becomes suddenly more bearable.

The pictorial symbolism that has been noted here and there in *The Friends* evokes a visual stage poetry almost as rich as the density of dialogue and of action. Esther, who alone achieves a sense of continuity with the past, is first glimpsed making old photographs into a collage "rich in brown, black and white tones and nostalgia". [9] Nearby is Manfred's unfinished model of the D.N.A. heredity molecule —heredity here signifying not an alternative shaping force to environment and choice, but all the pressures of the past, and, potentially, its value. From shops as symbols down to photographs as symbols, Wesker characteristically aims to point a direct relationship between an image and its dramatic significance. Thus, the shops are not chosen by chance to parallel the friends' attempts to create something independent of tradition, or to transcend and justify their social origins: the image is *there* to be interpreted in such ways, but it is also a direct *result* of particular, recognisable attitudes and aspirations, as opposed to, say, Ibsen's almost arbitrary introduction of the wild duck into the lives of the unfortunate Ekdals.

Wesker's play, as we began by saying, owes its richness to accumulation, and not only to the accumulative progress of thought. Wesker has united the poetry and resonance of *The Four Seasons* with the more recognisably social elaboration of his naturalistic plays, and he has created a whole that is greater than either earlier style could of itself promise or achieve.

5

Towards Totality

Fears of Fragmentation

ALTHOUGH NOT IN the strictest sense of the term a public figure, Arnold Wesker has been more prominent in public and political activity and polemic than most of his contemporaries in the playwriting profession—notwithstanding John Osborne's journalistic indictments of his critics and love-hate relationship with his country, or John Arden's increasing social consciousness as tentatively traced in *The Impromptu of Muswell Hill*. This more immediate and enduring involvement of Wesker's, whether in anti-nuclear sit-downs or in the cause of Centre Fortytwo, has been to his disadvantage in the arena of the commercial theatre, whose reviewers, often without seeming aware of the critical heresy they thus commit, tend to make each of his plays subservient to their own self-conceived portrait of its author.

Anonymity is an elementary protective measure against this imposition, and one that many writers have taken: but Wesker has always refused to resort to it, in spite of his fearful intimations of contempt for humanity. Indeed, he regards his public activities as an integral part of his work and intentions as a playwright. And so, in his case particularly, autobiographical parallels between author and characters are detected and castigated with something like triumphant relish: but of course it should hardly require repeating that such parallels are irrelevant either to one's understanding or one's evaluation of the plays as such.[39]

The lectures and articles by Wesker collected as *Fears of Fragmentation* form, then, a quite distinct body of work from the plays; yet they were evidently considered by their author, in his decision to collect them into book form, to be more than occasional or ephemeral pieces. And a discussion of them is useful here, in straightforward illustration of Wesker's seminal ideas, so long as the more tantalising echoes from the plays are not regarded as the sole points of interest, and the ideas in the essays not used as a short cut into the plays, or as more than retrospective confirmation of what is already and self-sufficiently in them.

Only two of the seven pieces in the book were originally conceived for publication, and these are both concerned with Centre Fortytwo—"The Secret Reins", an article commissioned by *Encounter* in 1962 which became virtually a manifesto of the movement, and "The Allio Brief", a letter to the architect who was to transform the Round House from engine shed to arts centre. The remaining five items are all lectures, and range from a talk Wesker gave at a student drama festival in 1960—titled even then, in foreboding of the trials of the professional playwright, "O Mother Is It Worth It?"— to the lecture from which the volume gets its title. This was delivered at the invitation of a group of artists in Tokio in 1968, and reflects Wesker's growing concern, most fully dramatised in *The Friends*, with the fragmentation of art from life, and of human experience from communality.

Among the rest, "Two Snarling Heads" was the address Wesker gave at the opening of the first of the Centre Fortytwo festivals at Wellingborough in 1961, whilst in "Tarnished Virtues and Confused Manners", a lecture delivered five years later in Stockholm, he offers a progress report on what he had hoped Fortytwo might become, and on its actual patchwork achievements. Finally, "Theatre, Why?" takes the form of a more personal statement, made to the Congress of the International Theatre Institute in Montreal in 1967, and can be read as a kind of prolegomena to "Fears of Fragmentation" itself.

Wesker himself, in spite of his insistence on the differences between himself and his characters,[40] denies that discontinuity between an author's life and his work is possible or desirable. Indeed, in a letter to the authors approving our refusal to join in a "detective-like hunt for the sake of satisfying curiosity", he nevertheless restates his belief that it *is* "possible to understand a writer's work against the background of his life". And this can be seen as entirely consistent with his plea for recognising the totality of experience, as expressed in "Fears of Fragmentation":

> I would like people to know me not only by my writing but by my life, to know not only *my* writing but the writing of my contemporaries; to know not only literature but music and painting also; not only to experience art but to know how it came about and the times in which it came about and what else happened in those times, and the currents of religion, philosophy and science which shaped him and the clues which there are for him to understand so that tomorrow's revolution will not be an ugly but a noble one. [128]

However, to *know* all these things is not to confound them together. And it is just because Wesker has refused the undoubted temptation, excused by authorities enough, to believe that "as an artist I can do no more than ply my craft", [44] that these lectures and articles, dealing with the translation of his beliefs into personal and public action, can supply a useful, complementary commentary on what the plays, too, are saying. Besides, the compulsion to buttress argument from personal experience is based partly on respect for consistency—a consistency that has been found everywhere in the plays—in this very matter of seeing life, art, the artist's life, the man who lives, as parts of an inseparable whole.

Apart from their illustrative function, though, Wesker's personal allusions (not that they are in fact very frequent or very personal) are intended to document his arguments with scrupulous fairness, and to disarm himself of the advantages of a "sincere" or pathetic rhetorical tone. There is a frank attempt to declare such emotional vested interests as are, say, concealed by those falsely dispassionate, secretly sadistic advocates of violence in the cause of civil rights Wesker mentions in one of his own examples—those who betray "a certain concealed pleasure at the prospect of violence". [119] Of course, if Wesker's audience is not capable of judging an argument on its merits, irrespective of its persuasive packaging, even this scrupulous restraint may be tying Wesker in further knots of double-bluffing rhetoric, for, as he admits, "the sight of a man full of doubts" is itself "attractive and reassuring". [65]

From Wesker's concern for the totality of experience comes the title of "Fears of Fragmentation" itself. As Wesker says, "this fear of fragmentation can be traced in my plays", although he himself was "realising this for the first time while writing this lecture". [112] And he instances how "all the time I'm anxious about beginnings, about complete histories", whether in choosing to open *The Four Seasons* with the lovers' arrival in the empty house, *The Kitchen* with the cooks' arrival in the empty kitchen, *Chips with Everything* with the recruits' arrival in their empty hut, or *Their Very Own and Golden City* with the young people's arrival in the empty cathedral. [113]

Of course, chronicling beginnings is a fairly simple approach to the problem of achieving completeness in art, a detailed exploration only in one dimension of experience— and this simplification similarly mars the title, but not the substance, of *Roots*. "The very title betrays an obsession with beginnings," says Wesker, [113] but in truth the play's dramatised concern with interrelationships in all dimensions, not just with going backwards in time—though it is part of a trilogy which does just that—is far fuller than his own admission suggests. However, as he notices, an anxiety to amass details, to give the full, true picture, is a technical symptom of an artist's more profound awareness of other kinds of connections. It is this awareness that the last lecture makes explicit.

In effect, then, these pieces substantiate what the plays themselves are saying—that the lives of many tend to be stunted because intellectual and social compartmentalising prevents the release of an individual's true potential, and that, on the contrary, it is necessary for

> working, playing, laughing, crying, eating, singing, dancing, studying, leisure and creative art to be not separate aspects of living, for separate people, but natural manifestations of the *whole* act of living for everyone to engage in and enjoy. [15–16]

As well as paralleling or summarising what is to be *found* in the plays, this set of personal principles *results* in the plays: the art of living crystallises into art *tout court*.

Art is in this sense considered as a key to life and as having "the function of stirring the human spirit". [35] But to underline the fact that this key should not be twisted to fit the cause of offensive didacticism, Wesker emphasises that art is also "a sort of hymn in praise of man". [18] His plays, too, both depict, in *what happens* in them, and embody, as his own marshallings of order out of chaos, the "desperate life-or-death pursuit for an understanding of the complex world we live in". [65] The belief in art that has made writing plays worth the trouble is, if you like, the hidden counterbalance to that bafflement one often senses within the plays themselves when characters go in fear of fragmentation.

It even seems that Wesker's crusade against fragmentation is for him the saving significance that insures against fragmentation—means and end all in one. But his very concern for unity suggests that judgements in the plays and the lectures will be based on considered principles and correspond because of this, not through caprice or coincidence. Thus, the flourish about children's comics in *Roots*—"there's nothing wrong with comics only there's something wrong with comics all the time" [87]—is part and parcel of the weightier attack on pop as "a phenomenon that excludes all else" in *Fears of Fragmentation*, and, in consequence, of Wesker's refusal to join in that "intellectual capitulation on the part of artists" towards it that occurred even in the few years between Beatie's words and Wesker's. [68]

There are many echoes in the plays as clear as this, and a similar consistency. But in the lectures the ideas relate directly to Wesker and to certain often topical matters that concern him, as well as to society generally—whereas in the plays the same ideas have a localised relevance and presentation. Thus, the statement in "The Secret Reins" that "all protest is allowed and smiled upon because it is known that the force—economically and culturally—lies in the same dark and secure quarters" [42] has the widest possible social application, whereas the identical import of the statement by the Pilot Officer in *Chips with Everything* has a close and particular relevance to the rationale of hierarchical air-force discipline:

We listen but we do not hear, we befriend but do not touch you, we applaud but we do not act. To tolerate is to ignore. [60]

Again, the suggestion in "Tarnished Virtues and Confused Manners" that "our cities should be built around our centres of art and not our town halls" [63] is an opening but subordinate point in an elaborate argument about artistic values: but in *Their Very Own and Golden City* the belief that "our city's heart is its gardens, concert halls, theatres, swimming pools" [66] is not illustrative of but specific to the play's subject-matter, the building of cities. The difference is one of emphasis and of method: in the plays, class attitudes and city are particular though also representative, whereas in the lectures their exemplary function is the most important.

Most of the phrases and passages that lead such double-lives are sea-changed from *Fears of Fragmentation* into either *Golden City* or *The Friends*, probably because a good half of the pieces were conceived between the productions of these plays, in 1966 and 1970 respectively. But the continuity of Wesker's thought extends back farther than this. The environmental theme of *Golden City*—there expressed in the belief that "in the way you build a city you build the habits of a way of life in that city" [59]—is thus foreshadowed in negative form as early as 1960, in the lecture "O Mother Is It Worth It?" Wesker then claimed that "the social and cultural habits of a group will continue for generations unless something is done to break them", and in both lecture and play it is through the Labour Movement that a solution is sought. [16]

The most resonant of these echoes do provoke us to pay more careful attention to certain aspects of the plays, in so far as they elucidate what is present but obscure in the text, or correct what is understated or overemphasised. In *Golden City*, for example, Kate's plausibly reasoned concession of industrial ownership and management within a co-operatively conceived city to private enterprise—"as if it makes much difference" whether the workers "own the machine or not, they'll still hate it" [79]—is less equivocally answered than it ever is in the play by the perception of William Morris that Wesker quotes in "Tarnished Virtues and Confused Manners":

> If they are determined to have masters to manage their affairs, they must expect in turn to pay for that luxury . . . remembering that the price they pay for their so-called captains of industry is no mere money payment—no mere tribute which once paid leaves them free to do as they please but an authoritative ordering of the whole tenor of their lives. . . . [80]

Again, it is not only Kate's "rational" attitude towards the city's prospective workers (or towards the victims of Nazi Germany) that is criticised by the warning that "so-called 'hard facts' tempt us to brutalise our compassion in the name of so-called 'harsh reality'", [105] but also Andrew Cobham's own fatal flaw and first wrong move in that rhetorical stab in the back aimed at Jake Latham, which he justifies by an insistence on these same "hard facts". Similarly, the muddled malaise of the protagonists in *The Friends* and their love-hate relationship with contemporaneity is diagnosed succinctly in this image from "Theatre, Why?":

> I have a suspicion that those who root themselves too firmly in the present are frightened of it. They force the disease on to their symptoms, rather than actually suffer with the disease. [96]

However, although the continuity and congruity of

Wesker's ideas and art justifies these helpful parallels between plays and lectures, it is still fallacious to explain away a biographical interpretation on this basis. For Wesker's plays relate to his life, as they do to "life", but not in any way by engaging in the frivolity of simple self-dramatisation. That is why the completion complex that compels his chronicling of beginnings, his worrying "in case a clue has been missed", [113] is not essential to the true "completeness" of the plays: for it is as self-contained parables that they must act upon our own lives. They relate by analogy—or rather, microcosmically, reducing to manageable yet representative proportions the intractable totality of individual existence. The way that the plays particularise the general truths of the lectures is, then, essential for Wesker to the artistic process—the crystallising of coherent dramatic images from the flux of experience.

Thus, writing of cultural revolution in relation to Centre Fortytwo, Wesker says: "We all have too often failed in patch-work schemes and accepted and retreated under the sneers of onlookers." [48] And patchwork is, of course, a keyword in *Their Very Own and Golden City*, which images in little, in its history of a city's creation, kinds of social revolution that must embrace and include the cultural revolution Centre Fortytwo was conceived to support. In the same way, the even smaller-scale ambition of the protagonists in *The Friends*—artistic education through interior design, offered to labouring fathers and tight-lipped mothers—mirrors the need of all reforming artists (and not only artists) who emerge from working-class backgrounds to "remind our working-class mothers and fathers" that, as Wesker puts it in the title essay of *Fears of Fragmentation*, "though we are a little odd, yet we are also their inevitable inheritance". [115]

The habit of image-making evident in these pieces demon-strates this happening at one further remove: from the brief metaphor in "Theatre, Why?" quoted above, in which diseases are superimposed upon symptoms, to the lengthier parable (twice repeated) of the dispossessed Adam and Eve who are taken over by the builders they hire to construct them a house, the choice of imagery at the same time sets forth and encapsulates certain meanings. The lecturer's method is the playwright's: the illustrations are more sharply etched for their distinctness from abstract argument.

When such parables are tied to one topical (or wrong) interpretation, the diminishing-effect of simplistic biographical clue-hunting upon criticism of Wesker's work becomes evident. For example, the early pieces in *Fears of Fragmentation* are concerned with the vicissitudes of Centre Fortytwo, in its original conception as an arts centre which was to function as a cultural reservoir for any client community. Its capital exhausted by mounting six festivals that left its freedom of action severely curtailed, Centre Fortytwo then acquired the Round House, the projected conversion of which would entail further crippling expenditure. Now the similarities between Wesker's involvement in Centre Fortytwo and Andrew Cobham's struggles for his golden cities are many in substance and verbal allusion alike. Instead of six arts festivals, there are six golden cities—but "them's also patchwork", and "all the Centre Fortytwos we may build . . . can only be patchwork" too. [79] Yet it is a truth so partial as to be tantamount to falsehood to say that *Golden City* "represents" the Fortytwo project, because the implication is then that it represents *only* that. Both ventures, rather, are equally representative of how things work in society: but whilst Centre Fortytwo is superficially continuous with that society, *Golden City*, discontinuous in its elevation as art, is and must be interpreted as self-contained. Meanings and even morals may emerge from it, but are limiting and constricting when imposed upon it *a priori*, by over-facile deduction from limited personal cause to in-exhaustible dramatic effect.

In the final lecture, "Fears of Fragmentation" itself, there is a shift away from the original concept of community art underlying Centre Fortytwo, towards a proposal for neighbourhood centres that would be as much people's universities as continuous festivals: and this shift perhaps indicates that Wesker no longer considers it the function of the artist to be at the beck and call of any and every town or village. Such a fortuitous relationship between artist and community may well have been instrumental in arousing the hostility of those who saw the Centre Fortytwo festivals as a swooping down of cultural missionaries, demeaning to the intended congregations. Wesker insists that he and his fellow-artists always waited to be invited—and it's true that, far from seeking pulpits from which to preach, they agonised over whether energies would not be diffused, as arguably they were, by accepting every invitation received. But the probably justified assumption that what was offered in the festivals was superior to the everyday fare available provoked accusations of paternalism, slumming or at the least patronage.

Such accusations are more convincingly levelled at the artist who comes into a community from the outside for a week or two, than against a resident artist, a local prophet who is happily bereft of suspicious honour in his own country. Yet the original proposals *were* rooted in a more sympathetic impulse than paternalism. As in Ronnie's education of Beatie, the greater knowledge of the teacher can elicit resentment—and encourage a *sense* of superiority such as Ronnie himself was evidently not above enjoying. But, if communication is a simple human need, how can anyone who believes himself possessed of truths or secrets of fuller living fail to hand them on if opportunity permits, and to seek opportunity if it doesn't?[41]

Wesker remarks, all the same, that this handing on, even in the relatively straightforward forms of lecture and article, is not too easy for the creative writer, because of the change of mental gear involved:

> It seems to me that artists should never lecture because the two activities involve disciplines so different as to bring about a conflict leading to paralysis when both are attempted by the same person. The re-creative process we call art contains an intuitive logic which it is not necessary to substantiate; the intellectual process on the other hand demands the endless substantiation of fact and figure, thesis and antithesis, qualification and definition: the unending accumulation of scholarship. To lecture is to marshal the knowledge accumulated by great scholarship. It is the application of one's intelligence to fitting together the known parts of the history of many things in a way that shapes a possible understanding of man's behaviour. On the other hand, to re-create experience, as the artist does, is to apprehend truths about man's behaviour from the small clues of one's personal and imaginative life. [109–10]

Usually, Wesker's own "qualifications and definitions" are deft enough: certainly, the distinction he makes here is a useful one, which illustrates one of the main arguments of this chapter.

Judged stylistically rather than thematically, though, it's true that Wesker's lectures are in many places singularly inelegant. Yet it may be ungracious to criticise the repetitions and syntactical convolutions natural in casual speech—or speech that is aiming at a casual, dégagé tone—when that speech is understandably less organised and impressive in reading than a text prepared for intensive and repeated examination. Moreover, as Wesker's own warning remarks about personal bias imply, he is bending over backwards to *avoid* being over-persuasive: "I confess to you a dream that reveals my uncertainties," he begins, in "Fears of Fragmentation", and the *wish* to confess is characteristic. [105] One is even tempted to suggest that in renouncing the rhetorical force of which he made Andrew Cobham capable, he is in part reflecting suspicion on that rhetoric, perhaps on all rhetoric, and so getting caught up in one of those vicious circles of the liberal humanist dilemma, all the more agonising for its self-recognition.

But this is not to suggest that one need even consider whether Wesker *as a playwright* is in danger of being afflicted by self-awareness to the point of literary paralysis. In fact—and this is an argument that has recurred throughout the present book—it is at this moment much more necessary simply to insist that Wesker *is* a conscious artist, aware of the ambiguity of his material and the problems of his craft. Perhaps in the end, among all its explanatory and corrective allusions, rendering such insistence superfluous will be the greatest service that *Fears of Fragmentation* can render its author. For whatever its faults of sense or of syntax—faults which, as Tom Maschler suggests in his foreword, contribute to our sense of knowing the whole man, imperfections and all [10]—it does set out clearly the process of Wesker's thinking, the progress of his sometime disillusion, the fluctuation of his hopes: in short, some of the sensibility and some of the substance, the streams of converging self- and social consciousness, that have gone into the making-up of Wesker's dramatic parables.

CONCLUSION

Conclusion

IT HAS BEEN unfortunate for Arnold Wesker's reputation that perhaps the most widely-read critic of the new British drama, John Russell Taylor, has remained so resolutely hostile towards his work. True, Mr Taylor, unlike certain of his more fashion-following colleagues, has at least been so consistent as to doubt Wesker's merits from the first. But his fullest and most influential assessment[42] of the dramatist, in *Anger and After*, far from avowing what he once considered a "quite notorious" lack of sympathy towards Wesker's work,[43] cloaks antagonism under the guise of a chronicler's objectivity—whilst the book's synoptic approach tempts him into serving up too many simplifications about plays whose cautionary nature makes them as peculiarly susceptible to damage from smoothed-over summaries of plot and character as from encapsulated value-judgements. Indeed, half-truths about Wesker's works tend not only to conceal but to contradict their untold better halves: and for this reason the dramatist has been as poorly served by the instant enthusiasms of his fair-weather friends as by what he has himself called, with some justice, the "casual condemnations" of more recent reviewers.[44] Indeed, the reversal in his critical fortunes itself suggests that the early eulogies should be viewed no less suspiciously than the later lamentations.

It is difficult now to think one's way back into the mood of the British theatre just after the production of *Chips with Everything* in 1962, when it was possible for one fed-up critic to claim that "to criticise Wesker as a dramatist would appear little less than a piece of sacrilegious impertinence, rather as if one were to judge Christ on his merits as a carpenter". On the evening of a performance of *Chips*, this critic went on, the Royal Court Theatre "is charged with an arch, self-conscious ritualism, a sort of theatre-going manifestation of the political palsy that has in recent years paralysed left-wing vitality into the posturing attitudes and narcissistic smugness of a fashionable prestige-cult".[45]

There is some truth to be distilled from these sour grapes: and yet Wesker himself, several years *earlier*, had also predicted the dangers of regarding the new movement in the theatre and in politics as a "fashionable prestige-cult". In a now famous letter to the *New Statesman* in 1959, he wrote:

> Here we are, having just started, most of us with only one play performed, we are just getting into our stride and beginning to learn about it all, and now some "fashion conscious" young smoothy comes along and declares with a bored yawn that "we've really had enough darling. . . ." We didn't set out to break down class barriers—no need to be frightened—we set out as artists and we haven't half started yet. . . . I didn't write *Chicken Soup with Barley* simply because I wanted to amuse you with "working-class types" but because I saw my characters within the compass of a personal vision. I *have* a personal vision, you know, and I will not be tolerated as a passing phase.[46]

This letter is important in several respects. It predicts, correctly albeit a few years prematurely, the passing from fashion which Wesker's work was indeed to suffer. It claims, even at a time when kitchen-sink "commitment" was at its height, that, in the long run, personal vision counts for more than mere contemporaneity. And it anticipates Wesker's own determination to stick to his guns and his opinions, whatever the risks of ridicule or of being written-off.

Paradoxically, this same letter was also one of the seeds from which Centre Fortytwo was to grow, as the making solid and permanent of a shared vision that would otherwise be fragmented and pass away—paradoxically, because in the very week of writing this closing chapter Centre Fortytwo, in the doldrums for several years, has itself finally and formally passed away. But whether its withering vindicates Wesker's feeling that the worthiest of visions will fade if treated as a seven-week wonder in the Sunday supplements, or raises doubts about the validity and viability of the whole enterprise from its conception is, of course, a different question.

It is not a question we intend to go into here. Indeed, the influence of Wesker's personal and political activities upon his dramatic writings has, throughout the present work, been regarded as the province of the biographer rather than the critic, and therefore touched upon only in passing. This attitude has been in some respects a self-denying ordinance, so close is the apparent connection between Wesker's life and his writings, and so tempting is it to impose conclusions drawn from the one upon the other—the death of Centre Fortytwo, for example, bequeathing only the Round House to the more trivial and compromising forms of living culture its stage had long since been reduced to offering, in this sense a belated, real-life equivalent to Andy Cobham's single, tarnished Golden City. And, of course, the clue-hunting critic could as well praise Wesker's vision in foreseeing so closely what was to happen to the cause to which he dedicated several years of his own life as blame him for its failures.

But the more apparently exact such a parallel, the more

dangerous the drawing of it. Andy Cobham declined into spiteful senility, whereas Arnold Wesker is still writing plays, his vision broadened but, in its essentials, not vitiated by the passage of time. If, in the years when political action seemed to hold out real hopes, Wesker *wrote* about political action, he did not underestimate the complexity of the problems any more than the difficulties of their solution. If, in the later sixties and the seventies, his characters appear to assume a political impasse, this is because the social circumstances of which Wesker writes have changed, not the vision that would have changed them in quite different directions. A greater complexity is thus inevitable, for there are two additional factors in the dramatic equation—the need to create a new *climate* for change, before attempting to effect it, and, underlying this, the need to work out some sort of personal adjustment to the mistakes and the patchwork achievements of the past. Such needs were implicit even in Wesker's earliest plays: and the Ronnie of the Trilogy, depressed but defiant in the wake of the Conservative victory of 1959, already had the makings—as the heredity theme in the play and the developing traits of the character himself combined to assert—of a middle-ageing Hampstead elitist not even bothering to vote Labour in the Conservative victory of 1970.

Wesker's vision foresees failure, then, even senses its inevitability, and in so doing manifests not so much that eternal fatalism of the Jewish sensibility traced by some critics, as the liberal-humanist awareness—in a tradition that stretches from Euripides to Ibsen—that a struggle remains none the less right for the near certainty of defeat. In this tradition, Wesker is perhaps closer to a novelist like Angus Wilson than to any of his fellow-dramatists. True, for Wesker there is always a scene in a soaring cathedral as an alternative to the hemlock, an insistence that defeat is no

more inevitable, however much more probable, than victory:
but there is also, pervasively, the recognition that the occasional victory is likely to be transitory, and maybe no more
than personal. Thus, the seeming shift towards greater
hopefulness in *Roots* is qualified by the downbeat conclusions
to the plays that precede and follow it in the Trilogy: whilst
the one entirely pessimistic work in the canon, *The Four
Seasons*, has *Their Very Own and Golden City* standing before it
and *The Friends* coming after, as if to temper its own cyclical
sense of futility.

What does, however, link *Golden City* with the concurrently
written *Four Seasons* is its uncertainty of setting: by contrast
with the control Wesker had exerted over the episodic
freedom of *Chips*, and the stricter assurance that was to
confine *The Friends* within four walls, the visual contexts of
the intervening plays now seem more imposed than integral,
a matter of sought-after symbolism rather than of found and
realised function. The rhythm of the *action*, and its reflection
in dialogue, has developed more consistently, however, from
play to play. Wesker himself acknowledges the guidance of
John Dexter, the director of all his plays from *The Kitchen*
to *Chips*, in orchestrating the non-verbal elements of their
actions: but whereas *The Kitchen* would be diminished
without its first-act climax of accumulative frenzy, the coke-
stealing episode in *Chips* is one among several ways of
predicating in the broader action the nature of Pip's ascend-
ancy—a splendid directorial sport, surely, but one which the
structure of the play permits rather than requires.[47]

At the time of writing, admittedly, it has still to be proven
in production that *The Friends* is as satisfying theatrically
as its text suggests, for Wesker, directing the premiere himself,
could not resist an author's usual temptation in such circumstances—to emphasise what was already self-sufficiently
emphatic, and to allow long stretches of his text to go

almost unpointed. This temptation proved particularly damaging to *The Friends*, since the play's density demands scrupulous directorial attention to detail if its riches are to be sensed, let alone fully perceived. It may, though, be that *The Friends* is one of those plays, such as Whiting's *Saint's Day* or Arden's *Serjeant Musgrave's Dance*, whose full import it is impossible to realise in a single performance, let alone at a first acquaintance with the text. This does not diminish its importance—indeed, *Hamlet* is of the same infuriating, fascinating family of plays—but it does mean that a production must sustain a certain added resonance, a tonal quality which is faithful to the play's full cerebral force, and at least reflective of those parts of it that it is virtually impossible to comprehend in any one single production.[48]

Quite apart from the faults of Wesker's own production, which any critic with access to the script should have perceived to be due to his deficiencies as a director rather than as a playwright, reviewers were further confounded by their own preconceptions. In expectation of a simplicity which has, in fact, never been more than superficial in any of Wesker's plays, they got unmistakeable complexity, and mistook it for mere cussed complication. As we have tried to show here, Wesker's work has always been more complex than it may at first sight appear—but perhaps it should be added that, *at the time*, the relative straightforwardness of the Trilogy or of *Chips* had its own rewards. The apparently polemical tone *was* appropriate to the late fifties and the early sixties— though even then it would have been more rewarding to glimpse complexities that, in retrospect, certainly told cautionary tales for those times. Now one returns to the plays, maybe merely in expectation of finding them period pieces—only to discover that, exact though their sense of period is, one's own later uncertainties have been anticipated. The failures and the doubts are *there*.

Maybe Wesker's earlier works will suffer, at an accelerated pace appropriate to our age, the same fate of suspected ephemerality that once eclipsed the plays of Ibsen—that comprehension-gap which, it seems, many so-called "social" dramas which closely particularise their time and place must suffer, before the old-fashioned matures into the historic. For there is no reason why the particular should not be permitted to identify the universal as sufficiently in *Chicken Soup* or *Chips* as in *An Enemy of the People* or *The Wild Duck.* Those plays of Ibsen's, at least, would seem equally susceptible to John Russell Taylor's charges—themselves mutually contradictory—that the didactic content of the Trilogy is too explicit, and its characters, whether Jewish East Enders or Norfolk farm labourers, too "exceptional" to be true. For few nineteenth-century Norwegian provincials could have been as exceptional as Ibsen's and few so apparently didactic in their creator's purposive eye. Maybe it's significant, too, that just as Ibsen wrote his most strongly localised plays in voluntary exile, so Wesker's plays have often been best appreciated in countries which are less concerned with the realism or otherwise of their minutiae, and more interested in what they are *about.*

Equally, the Jewishness of the plays can either be ignored or over-stressed. There is arguably a strain of sensibility that identifies Wesker's feeling for his own cultural inheritance: but overridingly there is a sense of humanity's common origins that makes this not a restrictive but a representative way of identifying a mode of feeling. And this *opening-out* of personal experience suggests the real importance of all the argued-over relationships between Wesker's life and his writings. Perhaps the most strictly autobiographical of the plays in this sense is *The Kitchen,* in that what Wesker was recreating there was a *rhythm*[49]—a routine and a pace of working with which he was intimately familiar. Or maybe one should argue for the greater truth-to-emotional-life of *The Four Seasons* and *The Friends*, impertinently suggesting that their intensity of "private pain" must hold up some analogous mirror to personal experiences of Wesker's own. Again, though, what matters even in such capricious clue-hunting is not ascertaining the exactness of the mirror-image, but perceiving *in the play* its reflection of a universal experience in the particular.

Even Pip and Charles, the male protagonists least liable to be instantly identified as Weskerian mouthpieces, have also been traced back by their creator to two sides of his own personality. Ultimately, therefore, one must be content with taking the biographical side-track only as far as is necessary to note Wesker's personal detachment from whatever raw material he may transmute into drama—and his greatest detachment of all from those characters, like Ronnie or Andy Cobham, admitted to have features in common with his own. It is this quality, incidentally, that has also helped to ensure Wesker's staying power as a dramatist, in contrast with all those merely competent writers of autobiographical inspiration, who may be capable of taking a total measure of themselves in a single play or novel, but who thereafter peter out their short creative careers in repetition or inept experiment.

Wesker's technique of characterisation—as distinct from its biographical sources—also matures from play to play: yet its outlines are already clear in *The Kitchen*. Its staple lies in the potency of what is incompletely revealed—at one extreme, in the narrow selectivity that sketches the officers in *Chips*, and, at the other, in the traditional psychological realism of the portraits in the Trilogy. Between lie all the characters whose actions and words are visible trappings to each one's independent—not merely dramatically necessary —personality. And Dave and Ada, Pip and Charles, Kate or

Tessa seem to live "outside" the action as fully as any of the more peripheral characters. The weight and conviction of Wesker's restrained yet close characterisation justifies itself: compare it, for example, with the claustrophobic portraiture of O'Neill, whose inclination is to put a character's every facet on well-documented display and then to *use up* each facet exhaustively as the motor element of his plot-making, so that a person's whole life seems to have been lived for the purposes of the play.

Wesker's less obtrusive technique results in the subordination of characterisation to the demands of the play as a whole. More immediately evident in the short-scened plays, his assurance in composition is manifest in the control with which he balances one block of action against another, so that character becomes just one unit of currency in a play's internal economy. Integrally, it is this counterpointing of the broad mass against the finer details of the action that embodies its meaning and, consequently, its value. The scene divisions of the Trilogy, less systematic than those of *Chips* or *Golden City*, are often split up again within themselves— as in the felt breaks in one scene in *Jerusalem* between the Libby Dobson and Colonel Dewhurst crises, or in that other in *Chicken Soup* which comprehends the solo-game, the off-stage disturbance concerning Philip, and Ronnie's return. This blocking-tendency points forward both to the closer independence between formal and conceptual divisions in the thoroughgoing episodic plays, and to the basically similar but less self-assertive hanging-together of the formally continuous plays, though the balance in the latter is (in these cases more appropriately) between one character, mood, or set of assumptions and another, rather than between purposefully contrasted segments of action.

As this suggests, the unity and independence of Wesker's plays is implicit even in their time schemes, which in the way they modify the total structure of each work relate to and reflect its subject-matter. In general, the more freely extended the movement of the play in time, as in *Golden City*, the more equably at least is the "possibility of change" weighed against outwardly stultifying experience. And the greater the tendency towards a closed, cyclical structure, the less credible does the possibility of change become. The more episodic plays are thus intentionally ambiguous in mood and meaning, their lack of formal pattern as non-restrictive thematically as it is structurally—whilst *The Four Seasons* is as fatalistic in its cyclical movement as in the statement of individual human frailty that its form universalises. Even between the apparently similar twenty-four-hour patternings of Wesker's first and most recent plays lies an important shift in emphasis—from the representative, repetitive pattern of *The Kitchen*, to the less structured but more specific period, spread in fact over a night and into a new day, which gives *The Friends* its more open and thus more optimistic ending.

But other developments in Wesker's technique and thought have of course occurred between his first and latest plays—at the simplest level, in his closer attention to craftsmanlike details like the management of exposition. More important, though, even than his increased technical assurance is the evolving flexibility of Wesker's dramatic language, which has led to an immense increase in actual and potential dramatic range. He has always been at home in faithfully reproducing speech patterns of particular classes—of kitchen or of barrack room—and of particular localities, from Norfolk to the fading north-eastern echoes of *The Friends*. But from *Chips* onwards the language of the plays shows more considerable and considered dramatic depth, and variation in *theatrical* tone—so that it acts on several levels beyond the fulfilment of its basic functions of being appropriate, informational and in character. Thus the compelling emotion, the evocation of mood, or the scrupulously varied rhetorical weight, that show themselves early on—in Paul's interlude speech in *The Kitchen*, in Beatie's reminiscence in *Roots*—help to underpin a more substantial proportion of the dialogue in the later plays.

Similarly, Wesker's concern with individual suffering, age and death—the irremediables of the human situation—is already evident in the early plays, though it comes to the fore only in *The Four Seasons*. That play's exclusive preoccupation with one year of very private life controverts any tendency in its predecessors to imply that every human problem can be solved by social intervention—perhaps over-defensively, in understandable reaction to the failures in critical perception that had caused the underlying doubts and the less dominant themes in *The Kitchen* and the Trilogy to be ignored. But in *Golden City* and *The Friends* personal and irrational factors weigh, if less obtrusively than in *The Four Seasons*, with much greater conviction dramatically. Pip's submerged, involuted motivation in *Chips* could—depending on how one unravels its ambiguities—be attributed largely to social conditioning. But Andrew Cobham's straight-forward lack of delicacy is shortly, simply and incurably part of his character. And, of course, in a reconciliatory and synthesising manner that bodes well for Wesker's future work, the dramatic movement of *The Friends* is from a massively depressed recoil against external pressures towards introspective emotional stock-taking, and back again to an individually-adjusted confrontation with external pressures.

But the most pervasive and unifying concern that runs through all Wesker's plays and draws in most of the other themes could hardly be more basic—the search for systematic sense in life, for an interpretation that is at least workably inclusive yet also life-affirming. The lack of this, though scarcely articulated, bewilders the cooks in *The Kitchen*,

caught in their enervating routine and groping in unresponsive isolation for an alternative. Ronnie's search for it, as
embodied in his political philosophy, is, it seems, close to
being abandoned by the end of the Trilogy: for him, it is
irreconcilable socially with what he experiences as an
individual—whilst for Dave and Ada it fails to offer even the
personal salvation it maybe promises Beatie Bryant. And
Beatie's problem has been precisely a rootlessness that denies
her not so much her rural inheritance as a means of grasping,
ingesting, co-ordinating and communicating *all* experience.
A fallen, sterile substitute of a system subjugates the airmen
of *Chips* in their faith-sustained, hierarchical world; and in
The Four Seasons Adam and Beatrice fail to live with and for
each other because they have failed to live with and for
anybody else. Finally, and most fully, the search for a
unifying order infuses the patchwork and fragmentation
themes of *Golden City* and *The Friends*.

What does seem to have changed is the emphasis: in the
earlier plays the central characters are baffled and dismayed
by the inordinate muddle of society, so meekly accepted by
its members, whilst, after the transitional *Chips*, the protagonists are aware not only of the confusion that surrounds them
in their sense of community, but of the dislocation and un-
predictability within themselves. To have sought to cope
with such a theme as this within even so tentatively naturalistic a framework as *The Friends* was to invite ridicule and
rebuke—just as the Trilogy, once its polemical appeal begins
to wane, may seem only overweeningly ambitious, and
presumptive in its ambition, alike to the enemies of its
ideas and to friends who sincerely doubt the usefulness or the
possibility of such a wide-ranging investigation as Wesker's
work actually attempts. It is, of course, much more accept-
able in the present theatrical climate to reduce a sense of
anguish to formal, laughable or intractable absurdity, and it

takes a brave mind to lay itself bare in a manner less allusively, more explicitly revealing. But because Wesker is
seeking to reconcile individual anguish with social anger, the
lonely lover with the golden city—and because, as *The
Friends* confirms, he believes that such reconciliation is
possible—he will probably continue to write plays which,
self-consistent without being self-satisfied, continue his
exploration from its original starting point, wherever that
may lead, instead of distorting his talents into the latest
modish mould.

As a dramatist, he will thus tend to suffer from temporary
shifts of critical fashion: but his plays will almost certainly
outlive those of all but a handful of his contemporaries.
Alike as dramatist and humanist, in concern for local colour
and universal truth, he is an Ibsen of our times—not least
in determining to write as the times require, not as they or
even his own inclinations entirely dictate. Hence—at the
practical level—the increasing number of drafts through
which some of his later plays have gone, before they have
satisfied a craftsman who wrote *The Kitchen* and *Chicken
Soup* quickly and almost instinctively, but who has since
been through a difficult, yet usually successful struggle to
keep congruous his thematic concerns and the formal shapes
into which they are to be fitted. That struggle seems finally
to have been resolved in *The Friends*: and this may well make
Wesker's immediately subsequent writing seem a return in
some senses to past preoccupations. For the adjustments to a
changed society—and to a self that failed to change society
along quite other lines—have now been made, and assimi-
lated into his work.

There will no doubt be other struggles, hopefully there
will be other reconciliations: for the present, however, one
anticipates a period of reflective work which may well be
broader in its social canvas and speak more closely and

allusively of its times than *The Friends*. This may—almost incidentally—enable Wesker once more to achieve conventional dramatic success—and maybe, circuitously, thus to create a climate in which justice can be done to *The Friends* itself. For, as the present study has consistently tried to suggest, the deep social concern underlying Wesker's dramatisations of private pain should be as richly rewarding for an audience as a sense of those personal struggles that temper the hopes and the failures of his apparently more public plays.

APPENDICES

Notes and References

Works of which fuller details are given in the Bibliography are here cited by their short titles only.

1 As John Russell Taylor has pointed out, the didactic episodes in *Roots* and *Jerusalem* occur at similarly climactic moments of each play's second act. See Taylor's *Anger and After*, 158–9.

2 In his review of the play's original London production in *The Observer*, reprinted in *Tynan Right and Left* (1967), 119–21.

3 "Theatre, Why?" in *Fears of Fragmentation*, 100.

4 Ibid.

5 In an interview with Simon Trussler in *Theatre at Work*, 88 and 95.

6 Ibid. Wesker thus describes the relationship between Adam and Beatrice portrayed in *The Four Seasons* as an inevitable development of his "concern with the problem of male-female relationships" in the earlier plays, and goes on to emphasise his belief that "one of the effects of art is to give people the feeling that they are part of a whole group, which is humanity, and to tell them that they are not alone, not only in any struggle they may make for a better kind of social world, but also in any kind of private pain and confusion and agony that they go through". Later he adds: "And this kind of private

pain, obviously, is very closely related to the forces behind the public issues."

7 One critic who stood aside from the general chorus of condemnation was Martin Esslin, whose approval may be of the more interest in that his approach to the play differs substantially from our own. See *Plays and Players*, XIII, 2 (November 1965), 40–1.

8 "George Devine was unhappy about it, and felt that I should combine the first and second acts into one act, and make the last act the second act, and write a new third act, in which Ronnie would appear. I thought this missed the whole point of the play. . . ." See the interview in *Theatre at Work*, 81–2.

9 Wesker himself offers a detailed discussion of the critical response to *The Friends*, the preconceptions about himself it typified, and the more general faults of critical approach it revealed, in his article entitled "Casual Condemnations" in *Theatre Quarterly*, I, 2 (1971).

10 The reference here is to John Russell Taylor's verdict on Beatie's speech in *Anger and After*, 154, reprinted word for word from the first edition of 1962, 149–50. In fairness it should be added that Ronald Hayman, in his own monograph on Wesker published in 1970, well after the Royal Court revival of *Roots*, did not feel that Bridget Turner's performance was comparable with Miss Plowright's. See Hayman's *Arnold Wesker*, 36.

11 See the Bibliography, below, for particulars of publication.

12 References to the text of *The Kitchen* in this chapter are to the longer version published in 1961 by Jonathan Cape. The text of the original version of the play was included in the Penguin collection *New English Dramatists 2* (1960), 11–61.

13 By John Russell Taylor, in *Anger and After*, 161–2.

14 Notably, of the Hungaria Restaurant in Lower Regent Street, and Le Rallye in Paris.

15 See the text of the original version in *New English Dramatists 2*, 61.

16 And it is *because* no answers are offered that it is difficult to agree with Ronald Hayman's criticism, in *Arnold Wesker*, 21, that Marango's question "generalises the implication in a way that distracts us uncomfortably from Marango's feelings to Wesker's intentions". The intention to pose a question is surely a permissible one, and dramatically more pertinent in this climactic position, than Marango's feelings.

17 But it is no *more* than a gesture—and is thus the earliest of those impotent acts of rebellion which Wesker has always found it desirable to distinguish from true revolution. "Rabble-rousers," says Esther in *The Friends*, "frighten me, they're only rebels, not revolutionaries." [46]

18 Her centrality, which Ronald Hayman also recognises, surely invalidates the premise behind his objection, in *Arnold Wesker*, 26, that "one of the weaknesses of the trilogy is that it is not only in *Roots* that Ronnie is more effective in his absence than in his presence". Once Ronnie's non-heroic status is recognised, this becomes a comment on his character rather than a criticism of the play.

19 And this steadfastness provides a "personal" parallel to the straight-line followed by the play "on the social level", which John Russell Taylor, in *Anger and After*, 149–50, feels to be inconsistent with the "circular" progression of the heredity theme. Such geometric image-mongering seems, in any case, of doubtful validity when used evaluatively rather than as a descriptive convenience. "Reconciling these two contradictory

movements" is more readily achieved dramatically—since characters demonstrably *are* shaped by events and by environment, as we have suggested, not simply by heredity in the Ibsenesque sense—than it is mathematically.

20 See George Eliot, *Adam Bede*, Cabinet Edition, Bk. I, Ch. XV, 230.

21 John Russell Taylor, in *Anger and After*, 156, doubts the authenticity of this idiom. "It is not, certainly, the standard mummerset that we listen to in the theatre, but neither does it bear more than a very superficial resemblance to the language spoken by Norfolk natives." As usual, Mr Taylor does not elaborate the charge, which it is thus difficult to refute, especially since one is no more aware of the degree of his own acquaintance with the language spoken by Norfolk natives than of his knowledge of restaurant kitchens. In any case, *need* the dialect bear more than a *dramatically* convincing resemblance to its real-life equivalent?

22 In view of this, it is strange that Ronald Hayman, in *Arnold Wesker*, 35, should feel that "Wesker, who is perhaps the only playwright capable of giving us a detailed and theatrically viable picture of how farm labourers live in Norfolk, is throwing away his chance of doing so"—especially since, only five pages later, Mr Hayman concludes: "Wesker is not only interested in the way the minds of the farm labourers work, he is able to characterise it both through what they say and through the way they say it." John Russell Taylor, on the other hand, feels that Wesker has been *too* successful in his documentation, and, in consequence, "does not manage to resolve that perennial dramatic problem, how can one present bores dramatically without at the same time boring one's audience?" See *Anger and After*, 155.

23 Ronald Hayman, in *Arnold Wesker*, 42 ff., evidently regards Ronnie as the central character of the play, since he scarcely mentions Dave and Ada in his analysis, and feels that the "unsatisfactoriness of the grown-up Ronnie" weakens the whole action. Again, however, this is a matter of character, not a symptom of poor play-construction.

24 See the interview in *Theatre at Work*, 88.

25 "Why shouldn't people eat chips with everything; are *pommes sautés* really preferable, just because to the genteel ear they sound better?" As before where Wesker is concerned, John Russell Taylor completely misses the point. It is Pip, not Wesker, whose genteel ear is offended. Why shouldn't people eat chips with everything, indeed? See *Anger and After*, 167.

26 It is for this reason that one doubts the force of Wesker's private special pleading for Pip, in a letter quoted by Ronald Hayman in *Arnold Wesker*, 58, which concludes that "Pip was not really concerned with power but he is tricked into believing he was." This would surely shift a burden of responsibility on to the Pilot Officer's persuasive powers which the conventions of the play ill equip them to bear. But there certainly is ambiguity here. One can only reassert the key to this footnote: what Pip *does*, in the last analysis, shows what he is.

27 See the interview in *Theatre at Work*, 90–1.

28 "I think that the characters of Pip and Chas are two sides of myself, but this is imaginative experience rather than actual experience." Ibid., 90.

29 Ibid., 89.

30 For the record, Wesker goes into these parallels in some detail in his first interview with Ronald Hayman in the latter's *Arnold Wesker*, 8–12.

31 "The form of the flash-forward gave me the opportunity

to cheat, to have two endings, in fact: the ending of the young people in the cathedral, which is still off the ground and optimistic, and the ending of the reality-stream." *Theatre at Work*, 93. "I satisfied that part of me which is constantly in conflict, that part of me which wants to encourage an energy based on hope tempered by the knowledge of the pessimistic possibilities." Interview in Hayman's *Arnold Wesker*, 10–11.

32 See the interview in *Theatre at Work*, 94.

33 Ronald Hayman, usually a perceptive critic of Wesker's work even when out of sympathy with his techniques, seems to miss the point here, or at least to reveal only a too-literal truth, when, remarking that "there are no other characters than the two lovers", he goes on to assert that, although "we hear a certain amount about their previous relationships . . . during the year, they have relationships with no one except each other." In so far as this suggests, as in context it does, that the play is solely concerned with this single relationship, it is surely too prosaic an interpretation. See *Arnold Wesker*, 72.

34 See the title-lecture in *Fears of Fragmentation*, 112.

35 One can see the force of Ronald Hayman's argument, in *Arnold Wesker*, 78, that "the essential element of physicality is almost completely missing from this love relationship". But arguably it is *because* of what Beatrice calls Adam's "waxwork passion", and the narcissistic nature of the couple's relationship, that any mutual awareness of physicality is thus dulled. [52]

36 See George Eliot, *Middlemarch*, World's Classics Edn., Bk. IV, Ch. XLII, 455.

37 See "Theatre, Why?" in *Fears of Fragmentation*, 96.

38 It's worth noting, as does Wesker himself in "Casual Condemnations", that Crispin's "it's true" here is not meant to intensify the remark that follows, but to

acknowledge it as a quotation, from Auden. Crispin, in short, is aware of the source, as well as Wesker.

39 It should be emphasised that Wesker himself regards the drawing of biographical parallels as permissible, and even necessary. See further our comments on this problem in the Conclusion.

40 He remarks in the first interview with Ronald Hayman, in *Arnold Wesker*, 2, that "most of the characters" in the Trilogy—"with the only exception of me"—are "total recreations" of real-life originals. But even in this extreme statement one notes the exclusion of Ronnie, whilst in the earlier interview in *Theatre at Work*, 79–80, Wesker also pointed out the important differences between other characters and their models—differences which, in *Chicken Soup*, "altered the details and the shape of the whole play".

41 "Nor did we ever conceive of 'taking culture to the workers'," Wesker insists, in "Casual Condemnations". On the contrary, "I had always known about this deeprooted English suspicion of taking anything to anyone so that from the inception of the movement we made it a basic tenet of our work that *we would go nowhere unless invited*." It is certainly time that the assumption that "taking culture to the workers" is somehow reprehensible were examined in the light of its unspoken corollary—that "giving" the workers what it is equally condescendingly assumed they will like, on television or in club, is somehow more honest and permissible.

42 One need only look at the single earlier full-length study of Wesker, by Harold U. Ribalow, to realise that Mr Taylor is considered, at least in America, to be rather more of an authority on Wesker than his published pronouncements would appear to merit.

43 In a review of Wesker's television play, *Menace*, in *The Listener*, 12th December 1963, 1001.

44 Analysed in the article of that title by Wesker in *Theatre Quarterly*, I, 2 (1971), 16–30.

45 See Frank McGuiness, "Culture With Chips", in *The London Magazine*, July 1962, 48–50.

46 See the *New Statesman*, 28th February 1959, 293.

47 For a more detailed discussion by John Dexter himself of his "five years of intensive collaboration" with Wesker, see "Working With Arnold", in *Plays and Players*, April 1962, 11, and "Chips and Devotion", in *Plays and Players*, December 1962, 32.

48 Material that has become available since this book went to press sheds intriguing new light on the circumstances of Wesker's own production. See "Production Casebook 2: Arnold Wesker's *The Friends*" in *Theatre Quarterly*, I, 2 (1971), 78–92.

49 See the interview in *Theatre at Work*, 90.

Arnold Wesker

1932   24th May. Born in Stepney in London's East End. His father was Joseph Wesker, a Russian-Jewish tailor, and his mother was Leah, born Perlmutter, who frequently supported the family by working in kitchens.

1939   Evacuated during the early years of the war, but returned for good in 1943 to attend Upton House School in Hackney. Trained in book-keeping, typing and shorthand.

1945   First attracted to the stage. Joined an amateur acting group.

1948   Began working at a wide variety of jobs, as a furniture maker's apprentice, a carpenter's mate, and an assistant in a bookshop.

1950   Began his National Service in the Royal Air Force. Organised a drama group for fellow-conscripts.

1952   On his discharge, accepted whatever work he could find. Was a plumber's mate, farm labourer's seed-sorter and a kitchen porter, before finding a profession as a pastry cook. Worked as pastry cook for two years in London, and as a chef in Paris for nine months, saving enough money to enter the London School of Film Technique.

1956   Entered the shorter version of *The Kitchen* in *The Observer* play competition. Saw *Look Back in Anger* and "immediately went home and wrote *Chicken Soup*". Lindsay Anderson read both plays, and brought Wesker to the notice of George Devine at the Royal Court, who passed the script of *Chicken Soup* to the Belgrade Theatre, Coventry.

1958   7th July. First performance of *Chicken Soup with Barley* at the Belgrade Theatre, Coventry. Received Arts Council award under scheme for assisting promising new playwrights. 14th November. Married Doreen Cecile Bicker, whom he had met when she was a waitress in a Norwich hotel. The Weskers have three children, two sons and a daughter, and live in Highgate.

1959   25th May. First performance of *Roots* at the Belgrade Theatre, Coventry. *Evening Standard* award as Most Promising Playwright of the Year. 13th September. First performance of the shorter version of *The Kitchen* at the Royal Court.

1960   4th April. First performance of *I'm Talking About Jerusalem* at the Belgrade, Coventry. 7th June. Opening of the repertory season of the Wesker Trilogy plays at the Royal Court.

1961   6th March. Off-Broadway production of *Roots* opened at the Mayfair Theatre, the first of Wesker's plays to be seen in the United States.

First performance of the revised version of *The Kitchen*, and release of the film version. Wesker imprisoned for one month with Bertrand Russell and others for his involvement in anti-nuclear activities in the Committee of One Hundred. Became Director of the Centre Fortytwo movement for popularising the arts, mainly through trade union support and participation.

1962   First performance of *Chips with Everything*, which

became Wesker's only conventional West End success when it transferred from the Royal Court to the Vaudeville Theatre, and of *The Nottingham Captain*, a documentary for which he wrote the libretto, conceived for the Centre Fortytwo festivals held that year under the auspices of local trades councils.

1963   Wesker's first visit to the United States for the New York production of *Chips with Everything*, which opened at the Plymouth Theatre on 1st October. His television play *Menace* screened in the BBC Television *First Night* series on 8th December. Began work on *Their Very Own and Golden City*.

1964   *Their Very Own and Golden City* awarded the Italian Premio Marzotto prize.

1965   Fourth of the ten drafts of *Their Very Own and Golden City* staged at the Belgian National Theatre. *The Four Seasons* premiered at the Belgrade Theatre, Coventry, and transferred to the Saville Theatre, London.

1966   London production of *Their Very Own and Golden City*.

1967   Wesker went to Cuba to direct *The Four Seasons* there.

1968   Wrote an unused film script for James Archibald of the novel *Madame Solario*. Delivered the lecture *Fears of Fragmentation* in Tokyo at the invitation of Japanese artists.

1969   Wrote the long short-story *Six Sundays in January*, which was published in the *Jewish Chronicle*, and adapted for radio by Vera Elyashiv.

1970   Directed the world premiere of *The Friends* at the Stadtsteatern, Stockholm, Sweden, on 23rd January, and the English production at the Round House in May. Wrote and delivered four instalments of *The Stockholm Diary* for Swedish radio. Publication of *Fears of Fragmentation*. Final dissolution of Centre Fortytwo.

Cast Lists

Chicken Soup with Barley

Directed by John Dexter. Designed by Michael Richardson. First London performance by the Belgrade Theatre Company, Coventry, at the Royal Court Theatre on 14th July 1958.

Sarah Kahn	Charmian Eyre
Harry Kahn	Frank Finlay
Monty Blatt	Alfred Lynch
Dave Simmonds	Richard Martin
Prince Silver	Richard Briers
Hymie Kossof	Henry Manning
Cissie	Cherry Morris
Ada Kahn	Jacqueline Wilson
Ronnie Kahn	Anthony Valentine
Bessie Blatt	Patsy Byrne

———

Directed by John Dexter. Designed by Jocelyn Herbert. First performance of this revival by the English Stage Company at the Royal Court Theatre on 7th June 1960, as the opening production of the Wesker Trilogy season.

Sarah Kahn	..	..	..	Kathleen Michael
Harry Kahn	..	..	..	Frank Finlay
Monty Blatt	..	..	..	Alan Howard
Dave Simmonds	..	..	..	Mark Eden
Prince Silver	..	..	..	Charles Kay
Hymie Kossof	..	..	..	John Colin
Cissie Kahn	..	..	..	Cherry Morris
Ada Kahn	..	..	..	Ruth Meyers
Ronnie as a boy	..	..	..	Michael Phillips
Ronnie Kahn	..	..	..	David Saire
Bessie Blatt	..	..	..	Patsy Byrne

Roots

Directed by John Dexter. Designed by Jocelyn Herbert. First London performance by the Belgrade Theatre Company, Coventry, at the Royal Court Theatre on 30th June 1959. This production transferred to the Duke of York's Theatre on 30th July 1959.

Jenny Beales	..	..	..	Patsy Byrne
Jimmy Beales	..	..	..	Charles Kay
Beatie Bryant	..	..	..	Joan Plowright
Stan Mann	..	..	..	Patrick O'Connell
Mrs Bryant	..	..	..	Gwen Nelson
Mr Bryant	..	..	..	Jack Rodney
Mr Healey	..	..	..	Richard Martin
Frankie Bryant	..	..	..	Alan Howard
Pearl Bryant	..	..	..	Brenda Peters

———

Directed by John Dexter. Designed by Jocelyn Herbert. First performance of this revival by the English Stage Company at the Royal Court Theatre, on 28th June 1960, as the second production of the Wesker Trilogy season.

Jenny Beales	..	..	..	Patsy Byrne
Jimmy Beales	..	..	..	Charles Kay
Beatie Bryant	..	..	..	Joan Plowright
Stan Mann	..	..	..	Frank Finlay
Mrs Bryant	..	..	..	Gwen Nelson
Mr Bryant	..	..	..	John Colin
Mr Healey	..	..	..	Anthony Hall
Frank Bryant	..	..	..	Alan Howard
Pearl Bryant	..	..	..	Cherry Morris
Postman ..	..	..	..	Terry Palmer

Directed by Jane Howell. Designed by Jocelyn Herbert. Lighting by Andy Phillips. First performance of this revival by the English Stage Company at the Royal Court Theatre on 23rd February 1967.

Jenny Beales	..	..	..	Thelma Whiteley
Jimmy Beales	..	..	..	Trevor Peacock
Beatie Bryant	..	..	..	Bridget Turner
Stan Mann	..	..	..	Billy Russell
Mrs Bryant	..	..	..	Gwen Nelson
Mr Bryant	..	..	..	Leslie Anderson
Mr Healey	..	..	..	Robert Grange
Frankie Bryant	..	..	..	John Shepherd
Pearl Bryant	..	..	..	Anne Carroll

The Kitchen

Directed by John Dexter. Designed by Jocelyn Herbert. First performance of this shorter version in a production without décor by the English Stage Company at the Royal Court Theatre on 13th September 1959.

Magi	Alan Howard
First Waitress	Jennifer Wallace
Max	Tenniel Evans
Mangolis	Peter Gill
Paul	Alfred Lynch
Raymond	James Culliford
Anne	Patsy Byrne
Second Waitress	Tarn Bassett
Third Waitress	Mary Miller
Fourth Waitress	Jeanne Watts
Dimitri	Charles Kay
Hans	Christopher Sandford
Alfredo	Jack Rodney
Gaston	David Ryder
Michael	James Bolam
Bertha	Gwen Nelson
Nicholas	Anthony Carrick
Kevin	John Briggs
Peter	Robert Stephens
Frank	Kenneth Adams
First Chef	Arnold Yarrow
Fifth Waitress	Ida Goldapple
Sixth Waitress	Brenda Peters
Seventh Waitress	Sandra Miller
Eighth Waitress	Ann King
Mr Marango	Nigel Davenport
Monica	Anne Bishop
Head Waiter	Cecil Brook
Tramp	Patrick O'Connell

———

Directed by John Dexter. Designed by Jocelyn Herbert. First London performance of this revised version by the English Stage Company at the Royal Court Theatre on 27th

June 1961. This production was revived, with a partially different cast, at the Royal Court Theatre on 21st August 1961.

Magi	Tommy Eytle
Max	Martin Boddey
Bertha	Jessie Robins
First Waitress	Jane Merrow
Second Waitress	Ida Goldapple
Mangolis	Marcos Markou
Paul	Harry Landis
Raymond	André Bolton
Third Waitress	Rita Tushingham
Old Waitress	Alison Bayley
Anne	Gladys Dawson
Fourth Waitress	Jeanne Watts
Fifth Waitress	Shirley Cameron
Sixth Waitress	Sandra Caron
Dimitrios	Dimitri Andreas
Seventh Waitress	Tarn Bassett
Eighth Waitress	Charlotte Selwyn
Hans	Wolf Parr
Monique	Mary Peach
Alfredo	Reginald Green
Michael	James Bolam
Gaston	Andreas Markos
Kevin	Brian Phelan
Nick	Andreas Lysandrou
Peter	Robert Stephens
Frank	Ken Parry
Chef	Arnold Yarrow
Head Waiter	Charles Workman
Marango	Andreas Malandrinos
Tramp	Patrick O'Connell

I'm Talking About Jerusalem

Directed by John Dexter. Designed by Jocelyn Herbert. First London performance by the English Stage Company at the Royal Court Theatre on 27th July 1960, as the final production of the Wesker Trilogy season.

Ronnie Kahn	David Saire
Dave Simmonds	Mark Eden
Sarah Kahn	Kathleen Michael
Ada Simmonds	Ruth Meyers
First Removal Man	Alan Howard
Second Removal Man	Charles Kay
Libby Dobson	Frank Finlay
Colonel Dewhurst	John Colin
Sammy	Terry Palmer
Danny Simmonds	Michael Phillips
Esther Kahn	Jessie Robins
Cissie Kahn	Cherry Morris

Chips with Everything

Directed by John Dexter. Designed by Jocelyn Herbert. First performance by the English Stage Company at the Royal Court Theatre on 27th April 1962. This production transferred to the Vaudeville Theatre on 13th June 1962, and was revived, with a partially different cast, at the Royal Court Theatre on 15th August 1963.

Corporal Hill	Frank Finlay
239 Cannibal (Archie)	George Innes
252 Wingate (Charles)	Colin Campbell
276 Thompson (Pip)	John Kelland

247 Seaford (Wilfie)	..	..	Laurie Asprey
284 McClure (Andrew)	..	..	Alexander Balfour
272 Richardson (Whitey)		..	Colin Farrell
277 Cohen (Dodger)	..	..	Hugh Futcher
266 Smith (Dickey)	..	..	John Bull
279 Washington (Smiler)		..	Ronald Lacey
Wing Commander	..	..	Martin Boddey
Squadron Leader	..	..	Robert Bruce
Pilot Officer	..	..	Corin Redgrave
P.T. Instructor	..	..	Michael Goldie
Recruit	..	..	Peter Kelly
Night Guard	..	..	Bruce Heighley
First Corporal	..	..	Roger Heathcott
Second Corporal	..	..	Michael Blackham
First Airman	..	..	Michael Craze
Second Airman	..	..	Alan Stevens

The Four Seasons

Designed by Zbynek Kolar. Lighting by Michael Northen. First London performance at the Saville Theatre on 21st September 1965.

| Adam | .. | .. | .. | .. | Alan Bates |
| Beatrice | .. | .. | .. | .. | Diane Cilento |

Their Very Own and Golden City

Directed by William Gaskill. Designed by Christopher Morley. Lighting by Robert Ornbo. First performance by the English Stage Company at the Royal Court Theatre on 19th May 1966.

Andrew Cobham	Ian McKellen
Jessie Sutherland	Gillian Martell
John Casper	George Howe
Jake Latham	Sebastian Shaw
Smithy	Bernard Gallagher
Kate Ramsey	Ann Firbank
Priest	Roger Booth
Stoney Jackson	William Stewart
Paul Dobson	John Shepherd
Chairman of Committee ..	Richard Butler
Official from Ministry ..	Jeffry Wickham
Alfie Harrington	George Howe
Reginald Maitland	Sebastian Shaw
Ted Worthington	Bernard Gallagher
Bill Matheson	Richard Butler
Brian Cambridge	Joseph Greig
Toastmaster	Roger Booth
Maisy	Janette Legge

The Friends

Directed by Arnold Wesker. Designed by Nicholas Georgiadis. Lighting by Mark Pritchard. First London performance at the Round House on 19th May 1970.

Macey	John Bluthal
Tessa	Anna Cropper
Esther	Susan Engel
Simone	Lynn Farleigh
Roland	Victor Henry
Manfred	Ian Holm
Crispin	Roy Marsden

Bibliography

WORKS BY ARNOLD WESKER

PLAYS

Chicken Soup with Barley. In *New English Dramatists 1*, Penguin Books, 1959; and *The Wesker Trilogy*, Cape, 1960, Random House, 1961, and Penguin Books, 1964.

Roots. Penguin Books, 1959; and in *The Wesker Trilogy*, Cape, 1960, Random House, 1961, and Penguin Books, 1964; and *The New British Drama*, ed. Henry Popkin, Grove Press, 1964.

The Kitchen. In *New English Dramatists 2*, Penguin Books, 1960; and *Penguin Plays 2*, Penguin Books, 1964. Separate publication of the revised version by Cape, 1961, and Random House, 1961.

I'm Talking About Jerusalem. Penguin Books, 1960; and in *The Wesker Trilogy*, Cape, 1960, Random House, 1961, and Penguin Books, 1964.

Chips with Everything. Cape, 1962, and Random House, 1962; and in *New English Dramatists 7*, Penguin Books, 1963; and *The Best Plays of 1963–1964*, ed. Henry Hewes, Dodd, Mead, 1964.

The Four Seasons. Cape, 1966; and in *New English Dramatists 9*, Penguin Books, 1966.

Their Very Own and Golden City. Cape, 1966; and in *New English Dramatists 10*, Penguin Books, 1967.

The Friends. Cape, 1970.

TELEVISION PLAY
Menace. In *The Jewish Quarterly*, Spring 1963.

FILM SCENARIO
"*Pools*: Synopsis for a Film", in *Definition*, 2, 1960.

SHORT STORIES AND VERSE
The Hill. In *The Jewish Quarterly*, Autumn 1958. Short story.

Pools. In *The Jewish Quarterly*, Winter 1958–59. Short story, reprinted in *Caravan: a Jewish Quarterly Omnibus*, ed. Jacob Sonntag, Thomas Yoseloff, 1962; and in *The Faber Book of Jewish Stories*, Faber.

Time Parts the Memory. In *The Jewish Quarterly*, Winter 1959–60. Poem, reprinted in *Caravan: a Jewish Quarterly Omnibus*, op. cit.

Six Sundays in January. In *The Jewish Quarterly*, 1969. Story.

ARTICLES
"Let Battle Commence", in *Encore*, V, 4, November–December 1958, 18–24. Reprinted in *The Encore Reader*, ed. C. Marowitz et al., Methuen, 1965, 96–103.

"To React—to Respond", in *Encore*, VI, 3, May–June 1959, 6–8.

"A Crucial Question", in *The Jewish Quarterly*, Autumn 1960, 43–5.

"Discovery", in *Transatlantic Review*, December 1960, 16–18.

"Art is Not Enough", in *Twentieth Century*, February 1961, 190–4.

"The Secret Reins", in *Encounter*, March 1962, 3–6.

"Director's Introduction" to the *Annual Report 1961–1962* of Centre Fortytwo. London: Centre Fortytwo Ltd., 1963, 2–5. Extract reprinted in *The Observer*, 7th July 1963, 19.

"Foreword" to *The Theatre of the Fifties*, comp. Sheila Wilson. London: Library Association, 1963.

"Art—Therapy or Experience", in *Views*, 4, Spring 1964, 44–7.

"Epilogue" to *The Four Seasons*, in *New English Dramatists 9*, Penguin Books, 1966, 188–90.

"The House", in *Encounter*, November 1966, 3–9.

"Delusions of Floral Grandeur", in *Envoy*, October 1967.

Fears of Fragmentation, Cape, 1970. Contains the following lectures and reprinted articles: "O Mother Is It Worth It?" 1960; "Two Snarling Heads", 1961; "The Secret Reins: Centre Fortytwo", 1962; "The Allio Brief", 1964; "Tarnished Virtues and Confused Manners", 1966; "Theatre, Why?" 1967; "Fears of Fragmentation", 1968.

INTERVIEWS

In Laurence Kitchin, *Mid-Century Drama*, Faber, 1960. Second edition, 1962, 194–6. Reprint of an interview with Laurence Kitchin, which first appeared in *The Times*, 21st September 1959.

In *New Theatre Magazine*, Bristol, April 1960, 5–8. An interview with Jill Pomerance, entitled "Question and Answer".

In *Challenge*, October 1963, 2. An interview entitled "The Future of Centre Fortytwo".

In *The New York Post*, 28th October 1963. An interview with Joseph Wershba, entitled "A Cultural Rebel".

In *Antioch Review*, Winter 1964–65, 492–505. An interview with Abraham Rothberg, entitled "Waiting for Wesker".

In *The Playwrights Speak*, ed. Walter Wager, Delacorte Press, 1967, and Longmans, 1968, 269–90. An interview with Walter Wager, which first appeared in *Playbill* in 1964.

In *Theatre at Work*, ed. Charles Marowitz and Simon Trussler, Methuen, 1967, and Hill and Wang, 1968, 78–95. An interview with Simon Trussler, which first appeared in *Tulane Drama Review*, XI, 2, Winter 1966, 192–202, entitled "His Very Own and Golden City".

In *Breakthrough*, ed. R. Goodman, Routledge. An interview with R. Goodman.

In *Behind the Scenes*, ed. J. F. McCrindle, Holt, Rinehart and Winston, 1971, and Pitman, 1971. An interview with Giles Gordon, which first appeared in *Transatlantic Review*, XXI, 1966, 15–25.

In Ronald Hayman, *Arnold Wesker*, Heinemann, Contemporary Playwrights Series, 1970, 1–12 and 81–91. Two interviews with Ronald Hayman.

WORKS ABOUT ARNOLD WESKER

MONOGRAPHS

Harold U. Ribalow, *Arnold Wesker*. New York: Twayne Publishers, Twayne's English Authors Series, 1965.

Michael Marland, *ed.*, *Arnold Wesker*. London: Times Education Services, 1970. (Times Authors Series, No. 1.)

Ronald Hayman, *Arnold Wesker*. London: Heinemann, Contemporary Playwrights Series, 1970.

CRITICAL AND GENERAL STUDIES

Max Andereth, "Sartre and Wesker: Committed Playwrights", *Comment*, V, July-August 1964, 18–28.

Michael Anderson, "Arnold Wesker: the Last Humanist", *New Theatre Magazine*, VIII, 3, 1968, 10–27.

"Arnold Wesker", *Current Biography*, February 1962, 43–5.

Mark Cohen, "The World of Wesker", *The Jewish Quarterly*, Winter 1960–61, 45.

Mark Cohen, "Impersonal Hero", *The Jewish Quarterly*, Autumn 1962, 48–9.

Nigel Dennis, "What Though the Field Be Lost?" *Encounter*, August 1962, 43–5.